Welcome to Let It Go by 3andB!

*We hope you learn a little to help
you live your very best life.*

- John & Lee

Discover more:

3andB.com

A very special thank you to
Katie and Cecily
for your editting prowess,
unending patience,
and loving support.

We would not be here without you.

Continue your journey by joining the
3andB community!

For more information on living your best life:

Website:
3andB.com

YouTube:
@3andB

TikTok:
@3andB.live

Twitter:
@3andB_live

LIVE SPEAKING EVENTS AT YOUR SCHOOL

We love visiting schools and speaking to students and faculty.
Contact us for more information about a live speaking event or
professional development for your school!

Table of Contents

Always remember your greatest Superpower is your ability to choose one thought over another; actively choose positive thoughts over negative to live your best life.

FOREWORD

We want to face any challenge or threat with a calm mind, cool body, and collected spirit. This is the goal of the Let It Go program.

As young adults we need to develop a strategy to deal with moments when we are challenged or threatened. This is necessary to not only live a successful life but to also grow. How we respond to any situation is a reflection of how much we have grown as a person and how we are able to control our emotions. Ultimately, how we respond to challenges and threats defines our lives. Do we rise to the challenge or allow the moment to get the best of us? Do we allow our emotions to control us or do we control our emotions?

Through self-reflection, trial-and-error and learning from our mistakes we begin to respond to different situations more effectively. When challenges make us feel like our core beliefs are threatened, it is sometimes really difficult to respond in a way that will support our future selves. Discovering ways to respond productively to these challenges is why we created this Let It Go program.

The origin of Let It Go came from the need to address our responses to challenges and threats that often cause us to "blow up" or "lose control." Social media is filled with examples of people freaking out over what appears to be small inconveniences in their lives that could simply be ignored. People of all ages do this, but why?

In our search for a method to deal with difficult moments, we learned the role the Defense Cascade plays. Defense Cascade is a different name for the "fight-flight-freeze" response that you probably have heard about in school. The automatic Defense Cascade that has served humans so well by protecting our ancestors from harm, does not serve us very well when we are dealing with modern life's moment-to-moment dramas. If we have any hope of improving our responses during difficult moments, we need to learn to take back control of our rational minds when our fight-flight-freeze instincts are kicking in. This is a lot easier said than done. Ask anyone unfairly kicked out of a class or in a disagreement with their parents.

Let It Go combines ancient and modern philosophies with scientific evidence on how to best deal with challenges or threats, especially in stressful situations. Let It Go aims to provide you with the tools to increase the quality of your responses to all types of situations. We hope these tools will allow you to have more positive responses in all circumstances.

Let It Go will allow you to maintain your best self in any situation, especially difficult ones.

Let's get started.

Why Sloths?

Sloths, not only are they adorable, but we think they embody some great qualities. Their wisdom lies in their slow and steady approach to life and how they don't let worries weigh them down. Plus, they are always up for hanging out! And have you seen the dance they do? 5 out of 5 stars, would recommend.

If we take the slow and steady approach, with consistent effort, we will see great results for our goals and aspirations.

Slow and steady with a carefree flair will get us there.

Open a book and discover a new you inside.

Chapter I: Introduction to Let It Go

Objective: High school students will be able to recognize and manage the Defense Cascade response by applying the seven steps of the Let It Go program in various real-life situations. Through this program, they will develop enhanced emotional intelligence, self-awareness, and self-control. This will ultimately lead to improved decision-making and well-being.

Chapter 1 Overview

• The Let It Go program is a 7-step approach to dealing with challenges and threats as your best self.
• Many interactions can challenge our beliefs and emotions, and it's important to know how to handle them.
• The Defense Cascade is the fight-flight-freeze response, which was helpful in the past but is not always applicable in modern contexts where our mental and emotional well-being is at stake.
• Learning to control the Defense Cascade response can help people remain calm and make better decisions in confrontational situations.
• The seven steps of the Let It Go program include realizing you're challenged or threatened, noticing your Defense Cascade response, breathing deeply, engaging introspection, becoming aware of the trigger, moving forward with a response, and letting it go.
• Let It Go can be used in every aspect of life, from small annoyances to more significant issues.

Video and Audio Resources

https://3andb.com/let-it-go-high-school-chapter-1-introduction/

Chapter 1 Video Introduction
Chapter 1 Audio and Article Audio

Readings & Activities:
1. Starter Activity
2. Chapter 1 Text
3. Chapter 1 End Questions
4. Chapter 1 Quote Questions
5. Chapter 1 Article
6. Chapter 1 Article Questions & Vocabulary
7. More Resources

CHAPTER 1 ONLINE RESOURCES

SCAN & GO!

CHAPTER 1 STARTER ACTIVITY: FIGHT-FLIGHT-FREEZE

Welcome to Chapter 1, where we will explore the Defense Cascade, also known as the Fight-Flight-Freeze response. This incredible system has shielded humans from harm for centuries. However, in today's world, the Defense Cascade can sometimes struggle to protect us from everyday stress. That's where the Let It Go program comes in. It empowers you to regain control from the Defense Cascade, enabling you to always respond with your very best self.

Fight, flight, or freeze? Is there a better way to respond to life's dramas?

Have you ever been so scared or angry that you had a fight? What happened?

_____

_____

Have you ever been so scared or angry that you ran (flight)? What happened?

_____

_____

Have you ever been so scared or angry that your froze? What happened?

_____

_____

In our hectic lives, it's easy to overlook the small wonders that bring us joy and fulfillment. But by embracing gratitude, we open our eyes to the abundance of good in our daily lives. Before diving into the Defense Cascade, take a moment to recognize and appreciate the people, places, and things that inspire gratitude within you today.

I AM GRATEFUL FOR THIS PERSON:	**I AM GRATEFUL FOR THIS TEACHER:**	**I AM GRATEFUL FOR THIS FRIEND:**
_____	_____	_____
I AM GRATEFUL FOR THIS PLACE:	**I AM GRATEFUL FOR THIS OPPORTUNITY:**	**I AM GRATEFUL FOR THIS THING:**
_____	_____	_____

"Between stimulus and response there is a space.
In that space is our power to choose our response.
In our response lies our growth and our happiness."

— Viktor Frankl

Chapter I
Introduction

Don't freak out! You have heard this before from a friend right before they tell you something that well, will make you freak out. Why do we react this way to some news? There must be a better way!

Each and every day our beliefs are challenged or threatened. Most of the time they are small infractions into our lives that we could just brush off. The person that carelessly bumps into us in the hallway. (It happens) The guy that has nothing better to do than talk trash all day about everyone. (Clearly has his own issues that he needs to sort through) Or a nagging teacher who is getting on our last nerve. (It probably comes from a good place, hopefully.) These are just a few examples of interactions that can and should be simply brushed off and completely forgotten. However, sometimes these simple intrusions into our lives can escalate into real problems.

How we deal with anger, anxiety, frustration, and drama that is caused by perceived challenges and threats to ourselves and to our beliefs is extremely important. However, most people (even parents and teachers) are not really taught how to control their emotions, especially in confrontational situations. Just being ordered to "CALM DOWN!" or "Stop freaking out!" does not help if you do not know how. So, how can we keep our cool instead of freaking out?

We can think of countless situations where people "freak out" and then end up with far greater problems than they had originally. How many times have we seen people at school get into physical or verbal fights? How many times have these ended up online? The internet is forever and some schools can take disciplinary measures for things that students (or faculty) post. Anyone that has experienced the fallout from this type of situation probably wishes they would have handled it differently. In the long run, it is often better to just let it go.

The problem is when we find ourselves filled with anxiety, frustration or rage, we tend to not make rational decisions. (This is what usually creates drama we don't want!) In fact, we make stupid decisions. We say stupid things. We make demands of people who have no power to help. Often, we end up hurting ourselves, the people around us, our reputations, and sometimes even our futures. Some people lose out on great opportunities, go to juvie (or even jail!), get hurt or even die because of the way they (or someone else) reacted to challenges or threats. We're usually worse off when we react without thinking. Choosing to pause and then act with all the information usually works out much better. We're worse off when we act without thinking and not taking everything into consideration.

It is likely that you have all learned a little about the Defense Cascade in school, or, as it is better known, the "fight-flight-freeze" response. While it may seem like a thing of the past that our ancestors had to deal with, it is a very real and operative system in all of us today. Many of us have not been taught how to control this ingrained survival system for modern contexts. The Defense Cascade was super helpful when our ancestors needed to run from huge, hungry animals looking to eat them. (Heck, it's still helpful if you run into a bear in the woods!) But it is not so helpful when somebody says something mean or posts an unflattering picture of you online.

Think of airplane pilots who keep their cool no matter how difficult the situation is at any moment. An excellent example is the movie "Sully", which is based on a true story. (Watch it if you get the chance!) In the movie, the pilots remain completely cool and in control, even after both engines are disabled by bird strikes. With no engines the pilots make an emergency landing in the Hudson River, just outside of NYC, saving everyone on board. Could they have pulled off an emergency landing that saved hundreds of lives if they had let their emotions take over? It is by remaining calm, cool, and collected that they were able to "work the problem" and save all the humans on that plane. Pilots are trained to maintain their calm, which means it is not an inborn talent, it is a skill. That means we can all learn it, too.

Few of us have ever been trained in dealing with life's constant struggles that test who we are each day. The subjects of human psychology and human behavior are rarely taught in school. If the subjects are taught at all, they are taught conceptually without showing students how to apply the information in their own lives. This leaves us to fumble through life, growing up and learning how to act through trial-and-error. It's a time tested method, for sure, but why do it the hard way when we have all this info that can help us? If you are reading this, then your teacher wants to help you learn how to support and maintain your mental and emotional well-being. They are looking to provide you with tools that a lot of adults never had growing up.

Each of us have difficult moments where we feel challenged or threatened. This is part of life. How we deal with these challenges and threats in the moment, as well as afterward, makes a real difference in the success of our lives. We have done our research, taken the advice of many, and used our own education and experience to develop this 7-step approach. Once mastered, it will allow you to deal with challenges and threats as your best self. Letting it go is a process. It might not be easy to do at first, but with practice comes great benefits. It is worth the work!

Calm mind, cool body, and collected spirit when faced with any challenge or threat, or dealing with any situation, is the goal of the Let It Go program.

Most challenges and threats (and our feelings about them) are temporary or transitory - they do not last and they probably will not matter in a week or two. Whether it is something important you need to stand up for, or a little thing that really gets to you, these 7-steps will allow you to maintain your cool with all the powers of your mind, body, and spirit at the ready. Let It Go will allow you to deal with the situation as your best self.

You can use the Let It Go program in every aspect of your life. Stub your toe? You could let it send your day spiraling until it is completely ruined. Or you could put the pain in perspective and Let It Go.. Someone cuts you in the lunch line? Sure, you could get upset and let it ruin your day, or apply these principles and Let It Go. Eventually, you can become instinctively aware of the power you have through Letting It Go.

The 7-steps are simple, but can be difficult at first. With practice, we promise that it gets easier.

On the following pages are summaries of all seven steps of the Let It Go program. Keep them in mind while learning the process for yourself.

The authors, John and Lee, have been using this method in their lives for some time now. The more you use it, the easier, quicker, and more natural it becomes. With practice, you will be able to quickly put challenging or threatening issues in perspective. We have found this to be an excellent tool to deal with the conflicts and dramas of life.

In the coming chapters, we will learn more about each step and how you can implement the process in your life to more effectively deal with challenges and threats. For now, we congratulate you on taking the first steps to learn more about how to Let It Go.

3andB
7-Step Process
to Let It Go

Step 1: Realize that you are challenged or threatened, a.k.a, mad, upset, angry, disappointed, jealous, or fill in whichever emotion or emotions that are causing you to feel mental anguish.

Step 2: Notice that your Defense Cascade response has been engaged and that your mind, body, and spirit are reacting.

Step 3: Breathe. Take a deep breath. Allow your breath to fill your body with energy and calm. This will disengage the Defense Cascade and allow your best self to reemerge.

Step 4: Engage introspection. As we learn more about ourselves, we understand why we are triggered.

Step 5: Awareness. Become fully aware of the trigger, as this provides perspective to learn from, change, or dismiss the threat.

Step 6: Move forward by expressing, suppressing, or calming your response to the threat, in a respectful, positive manner.

Step 7: Let It Go. Learn what there is to learn, place the entire moment in perspective, and Let It Go.

END QUESTIONS FOR CHAPTER 1

1. What do you expect to learn from the Let It Go process?

_____

_____

2. Do you think Let It Go can help you manage your emotions more effectively? Why or why not?

_____

_____

3. Do you think you could keep your cool like Captain Sully after losing both engines? Would you like to be able to remain calm like this in all types of situations?

_____

_____

4. How do you think keeping your cool pretty much all the time would impact your life and life experiences?

_____

_____

5. Can you think of a situation where someone has overreacted and hurt themselves or others? What do you think could have been done differently?

_____

_____

_____

CHAPTER 1 QUOTE QUESTIONS

Viktor Frankl is an Austrian psychiatrist and Holocaust survivor. He devoted his life to exploring the meaning of life and its links to happiness. Take some time to research Viktor Frankl to better understand his famous quote:

> "Between stimulus and response there is a space.
> In that space is our power to choose our response.
> In our response lies our growth and our happiness."

1. How long was Viktor Frankl in a Nazi concentration camp? How many of his family members were killed?

_____

_____

2. After experiencing the atrocities of the holocaust, why do you think Viktor Frankl was able to move forward and dedicate the rest of his life to the meaning of life and its link to happiness?

_____

_____

3. How do you think Viktor Frankl was able to overcome his tremendous losses and still find meaning and purpose in life?

_____

_____

4. How would others like Viktor Frankl judge your responses to difficult situations you have encountered ?

_____

_____

Staying Calm Under Pressure:
How Pilots Can Inspire Students

August 1, 2023 | 3andB.com Staff Blog Post
FOR IMMEDIATE RELEASE

Pilots are often considered to be the embodiment of calmness, even in stressful and challenging situations. This level-headedness and composed demeanor set them apart as exceptional professionals in the field of aviation. From managing unexpected engine failures to making emergency landings, pilots face a variety of challenges on a daily basis, yet they approach each one with a cool and collected mindset.

High school students can learn from the calmness displayed by pilots. Being able to maintain composure and make rational decisions under pressure is a valuable skill that can have a positive impact in all areas of life. Whether it be facing a difficult exam or managing a personal crisis, developing the ability to remain calm can help students navigate challenges with grace and confidence.

The Benefits of Remaining Calm
Staying calm is essential for making the right decisions in challenging situations. This is especially true in aviation, where the stakes are high. A calm mind allows pilots to think logically and make rational choices, even under pressure. Why is this so important? Let's take a look at the benefits of remaining calm:

Clarity of Mind
When we are calm, our minds are clearer and more focused, enabling us to evaluate options objectively and make well-informed decisions.

Problem-Solving
Being calm helps us work through problems by letting us accurately assess what is going wrong and what we can do to fix it. Pilots often face challenging scenarios and must find creative solutions quickly. They can better assess the situation by staying calm and making the right choices.

Reduced Stress
We reduce our stress levels by staying calm and avoiding impulsive or hasty decisions. This is especially important for pilots, who must remain level-headed in high-pressure situations such as emergencies or inclement weather.

Improved Communication
A calm demeanor also helps in communication, enabling pilots to communicate effectively with their crew, air traffic control, and passengers. In a high-stress environment, clear and effective communication can make all the difference.

Taking a Cue from Pilots: How to Cultivate Calmness

Cultivating calmness is a lifelong journey, but there are steps you can take to make progress. To become a more calm and centered person, consider the following:

Practice mindfulness and relaxation techniques such as deep breathing or meditation to help you manage stress and remain centered when facing challenges. Identify triggers that make you feel stressed or anxious and develop strategies to manage these feelings positively and productively. This could include taking breaks, seeking support from friends or family, or engaging in self-care activities.

Exercise regularly and maintain a healthy lifestyle, as your physical well-being can directly impact your mental state. A healthy body and mind can help you remain calm and focused even in high-pressure situations.

Surround yourself with positive and supportive people who encourage growth and success. A strong support network can provide comfort and stability, helping you remain calm in the face of challenges.

Take breaks and prioritize self-care. Whether taking a walk, reading a book, or engaging in a hobby, taking time for yourself can help reduce stress and cultivate a sense of calmness.

What High School Students Can Learn from Pilots

Everybody can learn a lot from how pilots maintain their calmness in high-pressure situations, especially high school students. Like pilots, students can benefit from staying centered and focused, even amid stress and adversity. To do this, students can practice mindfulness and relaxation techniques to help them stay relaxed and clear-headed. When they feel overwhelmed, they can reach out to their support network, whether it's friends, family, or a counselor, for help.

Moreover, students should prioritize self-care activities to maintain their physical and mental well-being, which can help reduce stress and improve their overall calmness. By surrounding themselves with positive and supportive people, students can create a stable and comforting environment that allows them to approach challenges with confidence and poise, much like a pilot.

In conclusion, high school students can greatly benefit from emulating the calm demeanor of pilots in high-pressure situations. By maintaining a clear and relaxed state of mind, developing stress management strategies, surrounding themselves with positive and supportive people, and prioritizing self-care, students can improve their overall well-being and approach challenges with calmness and confidence.

CHAPTER 1 ARTICLE QUESTIONS

1. What methods do pilots use to maintain calm during emergencies?

_____

_____

2. How does building decision-making strategies and effective problem-solving skills make you more confident?

_____

_____

3. How does having "clarity of mind" help you make better decisions?

_____

_____

4. What are some ways that you can begin "cultivating calmness"?

_____

_____

5. What can you learn from this article to help you maintain calm?

_____

_____

_____

DEFINE THE TERMS

1. Fight-flight-freeze response: _____

_____

2. Defense Cascade: _____

_____

3. Emotions: _____

_____

ADDITIONAL ACTIVITIES

Check out the 3andB.com website for this chapter, just scan the QR code below for instant access! Our website contains more information about everything we are discussing, including templates to complete all the work!

CHAPTER 1 ONLINE RESOURCES

SCAN & GO!

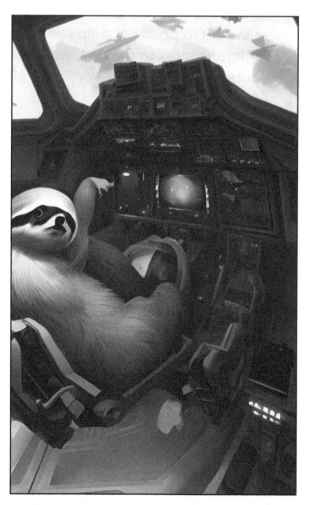

Remain calm, cool, and collected in every situation to perform your best.

Chapter II: Mind, Body, & Spirit

Objective: The objective for high school students is to develop a holistic approach to their lives by focusing on the three core aspects of the Mind, Body, and Spirit. This will enable them to cultivate a positive mindset, maintain physical health through proper nutrition, exercise, and sleep, and foster meaningful connections with themselves and others to achieve their full potential. Through the Let It Go program, they will learn to respond to challenging situations with grace, resilience, and emotional intelligence. This will ultimately lead them to live a fulfilling and purpose-driven life.

Chapter 2 Overview

- 3andB uses Mind, Body, and Spirit to better understand a complete person.
- Mind is the mental process guiding decisions and personal growth.
- Body refers to physical health and diet.
- Spirit is the connection one has to their inner selves and others.
- Let It Go program helps with responding to challenging situations
- 3andB aims to maximize all three categories, Mind, Body, and Spirit so a person can live their very best life.

Video and Audio Resources

https://3andb.com/let-it-go-high-school-chapter-2-how-to-use-mind-body-spirit/

Chapter 2 Video Introduction
Chapter 2 Audio and Article Audio

Readings & Activities:
1. Starter Activity
2. Chapter 2 Text
3. Chapter 2 End Questions
4. Chapter 2 Quote Questions
5. Chapter 2 Article
6. Chapter 2 Article Questions & Vocabulary
7. More Resources

CHAPTER 2 ONLINE
RESOURCES

SCAN & GO!

CHAPTER 2 STARTER ACTIVITY: MIND, BODY & SPIRIT

When it comes to our personal growth and well-being, three key elements come into play: our Mind, Body, and Spirit. Our Mind encompasses our mental activities such as learning, thinking, and understanding. Our Body refers to our physical health, exercise routine, and diet. Finally, our Spirit encompasses our life's purpose, including our relationships, goals, and aspirations. By dedicating ourselves to improving these three aspects every day, we can pave the way to success and live our best possible life.

Continuously develop your Mind, Body, & Spirit to live your best life!

Check the box that best applies to you!

☐ **I HAVE** thought about my life in terms of Mind, Body, and Spirit before!

☐ **I HAVE NOT** thought about my life in terms of Mind, Body, and Spirit before!

In your own words, define the term: MIND	In your own words, define the term: BODY	In your own words, define the term: SPIRIT
_____ _____ _____ _____ _____ _____	_____ _____ _____ _____ _____ _____	_____ _____ _____ _____ _____ _____

In our hectic lives, it's easy to overlook the small wonders that bring us joy and fulfillment. But by embracing gratitude, we open our eyes to the abundance of good in our daily lives. Before exploring the terms Mind, Body, and Spirt, take a moment to recognize and appreciate the people, places, and things that inspire gratitude within you today.

I AM GRATEFUL FOR THIS PERSON:
_____

I AM GRATEFUL FOR THIS TEACHER:
_____

I AM GRATEFUL FOR THIS FRIEND:
_____

I AM GRATEFUL FOR THIS PLACE:
_____

I AM GRATEFUL FOR THIS OPPORTUNITY:
_____

I AM GRATEFUL FOR THIS THING:
_____

"In three words I can sum up everything
I've learned about life: it goes on."

— Robert Frost

Chapter II:

How to Use
Mind, Body, & Spirit

3andB uses the broad categories of Mind, Body, and Spirit to discuss and better understand all of the components that form who we are as a complete person. The concept of Mind, Body, and Spirit has been around for thousands of years and, in this great tradition, we continue it today!

Each of us are made up of many components - a little of this, a lot of that - our own unique combination makes us who we are. As we go through this course it is useful to reflect on our life through the lens of these three categories. The concepts of Mind, Body, and Spirit provide a foundation for us to better understand ourselves and what makes us unique.

Mind is the mental process that guides our decisions, behaviors, and capabilities. Our mind contains all of our thoughts, desires, goals, needs, and wants. Developing the mind involves a commitment to learning and personal growth.

Body refers to our physical health and well-being, including fitness and diet. Developing the body involves a commitment to physical health, exercise, proper nutrition, and sleep.

Spirit can be defined as our connection to our inner selves, and those around us. Developing the spirit involves a commitment to self-reflection, self-awareness, developing good relationships with others, and finding meaning and purpose in life.

Lee's Mind goals are reading, education (both formal and informal), maintaining a positive mindset by selecting positive thoughts over negative ones, and, most importantly, writing and publishing ideas to help inform and entertain others. Lee is able to reflect on these components and make adjustments when necessary to meet specific goals.

For example, John regularly reflects on his physical health. For John, his physical health is made up of a good diet, plenty of water, and exercise 4-5 days a week. So under the Body category, John could say that his reflections on his diet, water intake, and exercise activities help him maintain a healthy state. By reflecting on these regularly, he notices areas that might benefit from some sort of adjustment.

John and Lee share many Spirit goals. These include being good friends and co-founders while helping each other meet their own personal goals. Creating and building a strong community of people working together to live their best lives is also a shared Spirit goal. Together, they uplift and help others meet their goals.

When you are proceeding through this course, think about how your own Mind, Body, and Spirit work together to form who you are. 3andB's goal is to help you maximize all three categories: best Mind, best Body, and best Spirit, which together will allow you to realize your best life. 3andB's Let It Go is our first program to help you live your best life by increasing the quality of your responses when faced with challenging or threatening situations.

We created a fun and simple activity to help you better understand how we use Mind, Body, and Spirit to categorize the many dimensions of our lives! Select the words that mean the most to you from the top and then place them in one of the three categories - Mind, Body, or Spirit - below. It is simple, and there is no right or wrong answer.

Each of us has a unique and beautiful mind,
body, and spirit to develop.

How to use the concepts of Mind, Body, & Spirit with this course!

Let It Go Mind, Body, & Spirit Activity

The terms Mind, Body, and Spirit have been used for thousands of years to describe the many elements that make a whole person. 3andB follows in this tradition. Continually develop your Mind, Body and Spirit and you will live your best life.

To help better understand how Mind, Body, and Spirit relate to the different elements that make up each of us, for each element below, place it in the Mind, Body, or Spirit chart on the next page. There's no right or wrong answer. Have fun!

Positive Behaviors	**Sleep**
Good Habits	**Relationships**
Financial Literacy	**Giving & Sharing**
Self-Awareness	**Finding Purpose**
Gratitude	**Work-Life Balance**
Higher Purpose	**Artistic Talents**
Skills & Training	**Exercise**
Physical Health	**Nutrition**
Teachers & Mentors	**Sensory Training**
Positive Thinking	**Family Well-Being**
Education	**Rest & Relaxation**
Problem-Solving	**Family & Friends**
Creativity	**Self-Discovery**
Healthy Diet	**Spirituality**
Being Present	**Living Passionately**

How to use the concepts of Mind, Body & Spirit

Let It Go Mind, Body, & Spirit Activity

For each life element listed on the previous page,
place it in the chart where you think it belongs best.

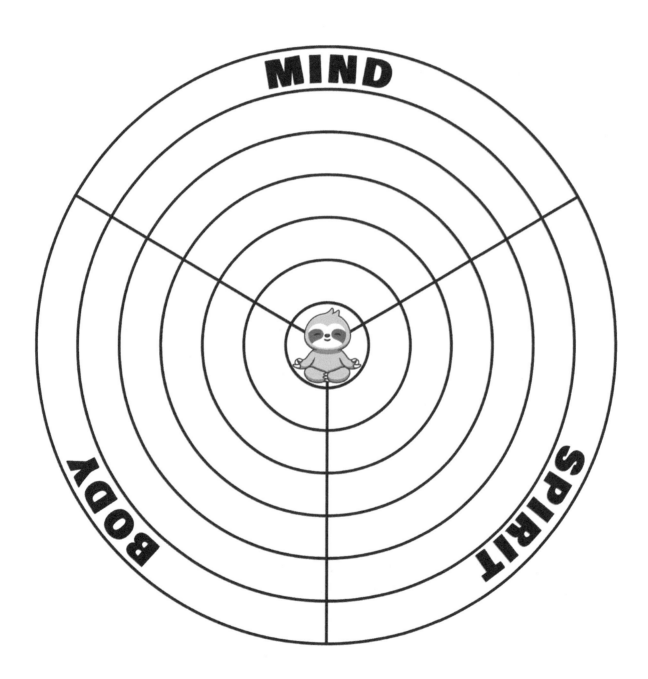

END QUESTIONS FOR CHAPTER 2

1. Why does this course use Mind, Body, and Spirit?

_____

_____

2. Describe Mind.

_____

_____

3. Describe Body.

_____

_____

4. Describe Spirit.

_____

_____

5. What are your current Mind goals and what are you doing to reach them? Think about your education, skills, and goals.

_____

_____

6. What are your current Body goals and what are you doing to reach them? Think about your physical health, exercise, and diet.

_____

_____

7. What are your current Spirit goals and what are you doing to reach them? Think about your family, friends, and your own happiness.

_____

_____

CHAPTER 2 QUOTE QUESTIONS

When the writer Robert Frost was asked what was the most important thing you've learned about life, he replied:

"In three words I can sum up everything I've learned about life: it goes on."

Robert Frost was speaking to the idea that when we feel discouraged we are tempted to say, "This is it. This is the end." However, Robert Frost learned that there is never an end, life does go on, and therefore, we should never give up.

1. Research the American poet Robert Frost. Who was he and why is he important?

_____

_____

2. Why is it important to not give up and to keep moving forward?

_____

_____

3. After difficult moments in your life, what do you do to move forward?

_____

_____

SOCRATES AND MIND, BODY, AND SPIRIT

August 1, 2023 | 3andB.com Staff Blog Post
FOR IMMEDIATE RELEASE

Socrates and other philosophers have used the concepts of mind, body, and spirit to refer to the different parts of a person that make up the whole self. This way of thinking about the self is centuries old and has been used by people to help them fully develop themselves to live their best life. By continually expanding the mind, body, and spirit, individuals can achieve their best life. This article will explore the concepts of mind, body, and spirit and how they can best be used to develop yourself.

Who was Socrates?

Socrates was a philosopher who lived in Athens, Greece, from 470 to 399 BCE. He is known for the Socratic method, which aims to increase understanding and knowledge through the (cunning) use of questions that encourage critical thinking. The Socratic method is a way for teachers to ask questions that encourage reflective and problem-solving responses from students. Socrates believed in the importance of self-examination and self-knowledge, which is reflected in his use of the concepts of mind, body, and spirit to explore the self.

Why did Socrates and many other philosophers use the concepts of mind, body, and spirit to define the self for so long?

Socrates and other philosophers used the concepts of mind, body, and spirit to encourage individuals to fully cultivate all three aspects of themselves. They believed that by focusing on the mind, body, and spirit, individuals could become more adaptable and achieve a greater sense of fulfillment. The three aspects of the self are both interrelated and interdependent, which means that neglecting one aspect negatively impacts the others.

How did he and others use Mind, Body, and Spirit to develop the self more fully?

Socrates and other philosophers used the concept of mind, body, and spirit to develop the self more fully by encouraging individuals to engage in activities that would cultivate all three aspects of themselves.

By choosing to commit to learning one new thing a day, a person can work on developing their mind. Making the commitment to walk every afternoon would encourage development of the body. The spirit can be developed by finding what you are passionate about and committing to it.

By focusing on all three aspects of the self, individuals become more well-rounded and can achieve greater fulfillment in life. This was (and still is) the ultimate goal of using mind, body, and spirit to develop the self more fully.

How are Mind, Body, and Spirit still used today?

The concept of mind, body, and spirit is still used today in various contexts, including in medicine, spirituality, and self-help. In medicine, the mind-body connection is recognized as an important factor in health and well-being. The connection between mental health and physical health is well-documented, with studies showing that stress, anxiety, and depression can negatively impact physical health. Therefore, practices such as mindfulness and meditation have been integrated into medical treatments to support overall well-being.

In spirituality, the concept of mind, body, and spirit is often used to help individuals connect with their inner selves and with a higher power. Many spiritual practices, such as meditation and prayer, focus on connecting the mind, body, and spirit to achieve a greater sense of inner peace and fulfillment.

In self-help, the concept of mind, body, and spirit is often used to help individuals achieve personal growth and development. Many self-help programs, books, and courses focus on cultivating the mind, body, and spirit in order to help individuals achieve their goals and live a fulfilling life.

How can we, as high school students, use mind, body, and spirit to best develop ourselves now and into adulthood?

We can work towards this goal by focusing on these three aspects of ourselves, we can become more versatile and achieve a greater sense of fulfillment in life. Here are some ways to develop the mind, body, and spirit:

- Develop the mind by taking challenging courses, exploring new interests, and practicing critical thinking and reflection.

- Develop the body by engaging in regular physical activity, practicing good nutrition, and cultivating a positive body image.

- Develop the spirit by practicing mindfulness and self-reflection, exploring values and interests, cultivating positive relationships, and finding purpose and meaning in life.

Closing Thoughts

The concepts of mind, body, and spirit have been used for centuries to define the self and to help people develop themselves more fully. By focusing on all three aspects of ourselves, we can become more well-rounded and achieve a greater sense of fulfillment in life. As high school students, we can use these concepts as tools to grow into happy, healthy adults. By doing so, we can set ourselves up for a lifetime of success and fulfillment. Socrates' wisdom continues to inspire and guide us on this journey.

SOCRATES ARTICLE QUESTIONS

1. Who was Socrates and why is he important today?

_____

_____

2. How has mind, body and spirit been used throughout time to help people better develop themselves?

_____

_____

3. Have you used the concepts of Mind, Body, and Spirit?

_____

_____

4. How can you use mind, body and spirit to categorize and improve your life?

_____

_____

5. Which do you think is most imortant to focus on, Mind, Body, or Spirit, or do you think all three are important to focus on?

_____

_____

DEFINE THE TERMS

1. Philosopher: _____

_____

2. Wisdom: _____

_____

3. Best Life: _____

_____

4. Meditation: _____

_____

ADDITIONAL ACTIVITIES

Check out the 3andB.com website for this chapter, just scan the QR code below for instant access! Our website contains more information about everything we are discussing, including templates to complete all the work!

CHAPTER 2 ONLINE RESOURCES

SCAN & GO!

Chapter III: Step 1 - Realize

Objective: The objective of Step 1 is to understand and identify the Defense Cascade, an automatic response to a perceived threat that can lead to irrational thinking and behavior. By recognizing when the Defense Cascade has been triggered, students will learn how to control their thoughts and respond mindfully, ultimately leading to improved decision making and emotional regulation in their daily lives.

Chapter 3 Overview

• The Defense Cascade is an automatic response to a threat that humans have developed over time.
• The Defense Cascade can be described as 1) acute-stress response, 2) fight-or-flight, 3) freezing, and 4) immobility.
• When the Defense Cascade is engaged, rational thinking is reduced, and thoughtless actions can lead to trouble.
• The Defense Cascade is an automatic system that cannot be turned off, but it can be controlled by noticing when it has been engaged.
• Failure to control the Defense Cascade can lead to problems in daily life as it was not meant to deal with modern life's daily dramas.
• Step 1 of the Let It Go process is to realize that the Defense Cascade has been activated.
• The Let It Go process helps individuals take control of their thoughts, react to situations mindfully, and with their best self in mind.
• Recognizing when the Defense Cascade has been triggered is the first step in stopping it.

Video and Audio Resources

https://3andb.com/let-it-go-high-school-chapter-3-step-1-realize/

Chapter 3 Video Introduction
Chapter 3 Audio and Article Audio

Readings & Activities:
1. Starter Activity
2. Chapter 3 Text
3. Chapter 3 End Questions
4. Chapter 3 Quote Questions
5. Chapter 3 Article
6. Chapter 3 Article Questions & Vocabulary
7. More Resources

CHAPTER 3 ONLINE RESOURCES

SCAN & GO!

CHAPTER 3 STARTER ACTIVITY - STEP 1: Realize

In Chapter 3, we will delve deeper into the Defense Cascade and understanding when we are in Fight-Flight-Freeze mode. Although the Defense Cascade can protect us in dangerous situations, it becomes counterproductive when it comes to resolving everyday conflicts. Many of us rely on the Defense Cascade to handle life's challenges instead of approaching them with a composed and collected mindset. Let's discover how we can navigate life's dramas more effectively by staying calm and in control.

Continuously develop your Mind, Body, & Spirit to live your best life!

How do you know that you are hurt or angry? What signs do you show?

_____

_____

Have you ever said something in anger that you later regretted? What happened? Did you later apologize when you realized you were wrong?

_____

_____

Who is a character (from a book or movie) that always stays calm, cool, and collected regardless of the challenges they face? What's their secret?

_____

_____

In our hectic lives, it's easy to overlook the small wonders that bring us joy and fulfillment. But by embracing gratitude, we open our eyes to the abundance of good in our daily lives. Before exploring Step 1, take a moment to recognize and appreciate the people, places, and things that inspire gratitude within you today.

I AM GRATEFUL FOR THIS PERSON:	I AM GRATEFUL FOR THIS TEACHER:	I AM GRATEFUL FOR THIS FRIEND:

I AM GRATEFUL FOR THIS PLACE:	I AM GRATEFUL FOR THIS OPPORTUNITY:	I AM GRATEFUL FOR THIS THING:

"The aggressive person fights.
The passive one runs away.
But the mindful person stands ground,
assesses the situation, adapts, and
acts with purpose and passion.

Be that person."

— Charles F Glassman

Chapter III:

Step 1: Realize

You are mad, upset, outraged, furious. You are angry and ready to explode. Where do we go from here? This is the moment where you need to realize that your Defense Cascade, or what is better known as fight-flight-freeze, has been activated. When the Defense Cascade has been engaged the parts of our brain in charge of rational thinking are far less active. Without the thinking part of our mind fully engaged, we tend to act without much thought. These thoughtless actions can get us in real trouble.

The Defense Cascade is a term used to describe the different defense responses animals, including humans, can have to a threat. Through time, humans have developed many innate, hard-wired, and automatic defense behaviors.

Broadly, these can be described as 1) acute-stress response, 2) fight-or-flight, 3) freezing, and 4) immobility.

1. Acute-stress response is the first step in activating the Defense Cascade: "I am aware of a threat."

2. Fight-or-flight is an active defense response for dealing with a threat: "I have to run!" or "It's time to fight and throw down!"

3. Freezing is a paused fight-or-flight response - I am not going to move: "I am frozen!"

4. Immobility response is the response of last resort to an inescapable threat: "It's too overwhelming. I am done for and I am passing out."

This book is not meant to be an in-depth study of the Defense Cascade. However, a very basic understanding of these principles allows us to understand why the Defense Cascade engages in the first place. According to the article, "Fear and the Defense Cascade: Clinical Implications and Management", if we want to control our response to threats, it is essential to realize that the Defense Cascade is an automatic system. The Defense Cascade has evolved for millions of years and is designed to keep us alive when under threat. Since it is such an instinctive and automatic system, we cannot just turn it off. Instead, we need to notice when this system has been engaged so that we can learn to work with it as opposed to letting it work us.

Why is working with it important? Isn't the Defense Cascade there to keep us safe? Yes, it is and in some cases, it works great! See a fast car approaching, jump out of the way - almost without thought. However, in our daily lives, allowing our Defense Cascade to run the show can cause more problems, like, a lot more. The Defense Cascade was never meant to deal with modern life's daily dramas.

So, how do we recognize the our Defense Cascade has kicked in? We might feel physical things, like our face getting hot or our heart beating really fast or it might be more in our head, like really intense judgements screaming through like race cars. Or we might feel like we can not think or move at all.

Someone said or did something that made you mad, made you furious. Every single one of us has been there. Now is the time to realize that you are entering the Defense Cascade. This moment is the hardest to gain control over. It is the moment when crap hits the fan, the sense of injustice overwhelms you, and you see red. This is when you need to realize that you are in the Defense Cascade, and you are in deep. This realization takes practice. Sometimes, it takes a lot of practice. But once you can notice it in the moment, you have the ability to control it!

For now, just think about the fact that when we face things we perceive as threats, our first reaction is probably part of the Defense Cascade response and we do not make great decisions in that headspace. Step 2 will help us identify when the Defense Cascade is engaging by noticing the very real changes that occur to our Mind, Body, and Spirit.

Now, let's do a mental exercise! Remember a time when you felt wronged to the point where anger, frustration, anxiety, or fear just took over. It is at this moment that our Defense Cascade may engage. In every single one of our cells, there is DNA that programs our body's responses to these kinds of situations. As our adrenaline builds and our Defense Cascade engages, we react without much thought. Instead of rationally making an argument, we scream, yell, cry, or break down. This ingrained instinct is why it can be really hard to take control. Being able to recognize that it is happening in the moment is a kind of superpower that we are all capable of.

All of us marvel at the character in the movie who, in the face of extreme adversity, is totally chill, capable and in control. Successful people, especially in business or even politics, have learned to control their emotional responses. The phrase "never let them see you sweat" might come to mind. Think back to the example of Captain Sully who remained calm, cool, and collected while landing a powerless jet in the Hudson River. While we cannot teach you how to fly a plane, we can definitely help you get into that hero mindset. Learning the Let It Go process is the first step.

When triggered, practice self-recognition by saying to yourself, "I am getting mad, I am getting triggered." That is all there is to Step 1! This is the first step to taking control of your thoughts. Realizing when you are triggered is the very first step in stopping your Defense Cascade. With time and practice, this will lead you toward actively responding to all sorts of situations in a mindful, appropriate way. We want you to learn to react with your best self: your mind calm, your body cool, and your spirit collected.

In our next activity, we'll ask you to make a list of a few times when your Defense Cascade was activated and what the outcome was. Be honest with yourself! The more honest you are, the more you will gain. This process will help you realize when you are in the Defense Cascade, which will allow you to start taking back control.

Recognizing when our Defense Cascade is triggered, by mentally noting when you are getting mad, stressed, anxious etc. is all there is to Step 1. Now that we have covered Step 1, Step 2 will help us realize that we have been triggered by taking notice of how our Mind, Body, and Spirit are reacting to our Defense Cascade engaging.

When Was Your Defense Cascade Engaged?

Think back to a time when your Defense Cascade was activated. Let's analyze the antecedent (what triggered the Defense Cascade), your behavior (what was your reaction), and the consequence (what was the result) of your reaction.

Analysis 1: When was your Defense Cascade engaged?

What triggered your Defense Dascade? (What happened before?)

Describe your behavior while your Defense Cascade was engaged?

What were the consequences of your reaction? Did you hurt yourself or others?

Analysis 2: When was your Defense Cascade engaged?

What triggered your Defense Cascade? (What happened before?)

Describe your behavior while your Defense Cascade was engaged?

What were the consequences of your reaction? Did you hurt yourself or others?

When Was Your Defense Cascade Engaged?

LET IT GO: Activity #1 Continued

Analysis 3: When was your Defense Cascade engaged?

What triggered your Defense Cascade? (What happened before?)

Describe your behavior while your Defense Cascade was engaged?

What were the consequences of your reaction? Did you hurt yourself or others?

What words are you going to start saying to yourself when you REALIZE you are being triggered and your Defense Cascade is engaging?

_____

_____

_____

_____

END QUESTIONS FOR CHAPTER 3

1. What is the Defense Cascade?

_____

_____

2. Why is it so hard to gain control over the Defense Cascade?

_____

_____

3. Why might the Defense Cascade not be a good way to deal with life's daily dramas?

_____

_____

4. What is the first step in the Let It Go process?

_____

_____

5. In Step 1, what should we do when we realize our Defense Cascade is engaging?

_____

_____

CHAPTER 3 QUOTE QUESTIONS

Dr. Charles Glassman is an American Medical Doctor with over 25 years of experience working with patients to help them live their very best lives. He believes that negative thoughts and responses are the biggest obstacles to each of us living our best lives. His famous quote is below:

> "The aggressive person fights.
> The passive one runs away.
> But the mindful person stands ground,
> assesses the situation, adapts, and
> acts with purpose and passion.
>
> Be that person."

1. How does the mindful person act differently than the aggressive or passive person?

_____

_____

2. What kind of person does Dr. Glassman want you to be?

_____

_____

3. What does acting with purpose and passion mean?

_____

_____

4, How can you start acting more mindfully and purposefully?

_____

_____

THE DEFENSE CASCADE CAN MAKE A MOUNTAIN OUT OF A MOLEHILL

August 1, 2023 | 3andB.com Staff Blog Post
FOR IMMEDIATE RELEASE

Once upon a time, getting eaten by a dangerous beastie was a daily possibility—can you imagine? For millions of years, humans evolved in a world where lions, tigers, and bears were a constant threat, and as a result, the Defense Cascade was born (also known as the Fight-Flight-Freeze Response).

But here's the problem, becoming the snack of a wild animal isn't something we typically have to worry about anymore. Instead of lions, the Defense Cascade is being triggered by life's daily dramas, turning minor social problems into major life-or-death reactions, and that can have serious consequences.

So, let's take a closer look at the Defense Cascade and talk about what can happen if you let it control your life and how you can deal with it.

Understanding the Defense Cascade

The Defense Cascade developed to protect our physical existence. When trouble arises, our brains analyze the situation and decide what action is needed—fight, flight, or freeze. In a matter of seconds, our body preps us for immediate action by increasing our heart rate, speeding up our breathing, oxygenating our blood while directing it to major muscle groups. All these changes enhance our senses so we are ready to react fast!

These physical responses are only supposed to last about 20 to 30 minutes—just long enough to get away from danger. You've likely experienced the Defense Cascade while coming across a vicious dog, being in a physical altercation, or having a friend jump out and scare you. (Aren't friends just great?) It's a natural process that keeps us safe, but it can be overactive.

Running from Imaginary Lions

What's happening in today's world is that the Defense Cascade is also becoming our response to problems that don't threaten our physical existence. The kind of defense options it gives doesn't really help us with non-physical threats. For example, the fear of not getting enough likes on Instagram, having your parents embarrass you in public, or not having a date to the dance can trigger the same Fight-Flight-Freeze Response that used to help us avoid being eaten.

If you allow the Defense Cascade to control your reactions to daily life, well then, your body will be in a constant state of running from imaginary lions. That constant level of stress can have some powerful consequences on your mental and physical health.

Consequences of the Defense Cascade

When the Defense Cascade doesn't switch off, fear takes control of our lives. Chronic stress can have several physical side effects, such as a lowered immune system, loss of appetite, and weight gain. But it doesn't stop there. Your mental health also takes a serious hit as anxiety and depression become your norm.

Over time, if you don't take back control, you can fall into a state of learned helplessness, resulting in a lack of motivation and the belief that it's impossible to change stressful or negative situations—that's not a good place to be!

So, what in the world can you do about it?

Learning to Let It Go

The good news is that you don't have to let the Defense Cascade dictate your life—imaginary lions are just imaginary, after all. Being able to put things in perspective allows us to manage our stress response in a healthy way. Nobody wants to be the person that leaves the house with their shirt on backwards, their fly open, or with stuff in their teeth, but will it actually end the world? Probably not. Just fix it, maybe laugh about it a bit with your friends and get on with your day.

Learning to overcome our fight-flight-freeze response will give us greater control over our reactions in all situations.

Learning to see situations for what they really are takes time and practice, but you can do it. The next time you feel the Defense Cascade kicking in, ask yourself: Am I about to be eaten by a wild animal, or is my brain just tricking me? Chances are it's just your brain tricking you—at least we hope so!

DEFENSE CASCADE ARTICLE QUESTIONS

1. How can the Defense Cascade turn a seemingly small problem into a big problem?

_____

_____

2. What are some situations that you might consider stressful and would not be solved by responding with fight or flight?

_____

_____

3. What does the article mean by "running from imaginary lions"?

_____

_____

4. Have you ever had an experience where the Defense Cascade helped you stay safe? How did it help you?

_____

_____

5. Why is it important to learn how to control your Defense Cascade?

_____

_____

DEFINE AND DESCRIBE

1. What is acute-stress response in terms of the Defense Cascade?

_____

_____

2. What is fight-or-flight in terms of the Defense Cascade?

_____

_____

3. What is freezing in terms of the Defense Cascade?

_____

_____

4. What is the immobility response in terms of the Defense Cascade?

_____

_____

ADDITIONAL ACTIVITIES

Check out the 3andB.com website for this chapter, just scan the QR code for instant access! Our website contains more information about everything we are discussing, including templates to complete all the work!

CHAPTER 3 ONLINE RESOURCES

SCAN & GO!

Chapter IV: Step 2 - Notice

Objective: The objective of Step 2 is to recognize changes happening in your mind, body, and spirit that indicate your Defense Cascade is activating. This includes identifying physiological changes, understanding basic emotions, and being aware of non-physical threats that can trigger Defense Cascade responses.

Chapter 4 Overview

- The goal of Step 2 is to notice changes happening in the mind, body, and spirit, which can act as a warning that the Defense Cascade is engaging.
- Physiological changes, such as increased heart rate and blood pressure, are triggered by hormones released by the adrenal glands.
- Dr. Robert Plutchik identified six basic emotions: sadness, happiness, fear, anger, surprise, and disgust.
- Being able to identify and categorize emotions can help understand reactions in different situations.
- Non-physical threats, such as interpersonal rejections, can trigger Defense Cascade responses.
- Step 2 involves noticing reactions to feeling threatened or challenged, including physical and emotional changes in the mind, body, and spirit.
- Mastering Step 2 takes practice, but learning to notice the signs of the Defense Cascade can help prevent automatic and potentially damaging reactions.

Video and Audio Resources

https://3andb.com/let-it-go-high-school-chapter-4-step-2-notice/

Chapter 4 Video Introduction
Chapter 4 Audio and Article Audio

Readings & Activities:
1. Starter Activity
2. Chapter 4 Text
3. Chapter 4 End Questions
4. Chapter 4 Quote Questions
5. Chapter 4 Article
6. Chapter 4 Article Questions & Vocabulary
7. More Resources

CHAPTER 4 ONLINE RESOURCES

SCAN & GO!

CHAPTER 4 STARTER ACTIVITY: STEP 2 - NOTICE

Chapter 4 delves into the powerful impact of the Defense Cascade on our Mind, Body, and Spirit. When the Defense Cascade is triggered, our entire being gears up to fight, run, or freeze. By being aware of the actual shifts that happen to our Mind, Body, and Spirit, we gain valuable insights to regain control. Discovering how you personally react to the Defense Cascade's activation will enhance your understanding of your own responses.

Continuously develop your Mind, Body, & Spirit to live your best life!

Check the box that best applies to you!

☐ **I ALWAYS** remain calm, cool, and collected, even in difficult moments.

☐ **I DO NOT ALWAYS** remain calm, cool, and collected, in difficult moments.

How does my MIND react when I am upset or angry?	**How does my BODY react when I am upset or angry?**	**How does my SPIRIT react when I am upset or angry?**
_____ _____ _____ _____ _____	_____ _____ _____ _____ _____	_____ _____ _____ _____ _____

In our hectic lives, it's easy to overlook the small wonders that bring us joy and fulfillment. But by embracing gratitude, we open our eyes to the abundance of good in our daily lives. Before exploring Step 2, take a moment to recognize and appreciate the people, places, and things that inspire gratitude within you today.

I AM GRATEFUL FOR THIS PERSON:	**I AM GRATEFUL FOR THIS TEACHER:**	**I AM GRATEFUL FOR THIS FRIEND:**
_____	_____	_____

I AM GRATEFUL FOR THIS PLACE:	**I AM GRATEFUL FOR THIS OPPORTUNITY:**	**I AM GRATEFUL FOR THIS THING:**
_____	_____	_____

"Stress is the trash of modern life – we all generate it,
but if you don't dispose of it properly,
it will pile up and overtake your life."

— Danzae Pace

Chapter IV

Step 2: Notice

When the Defense Cascade engages, our entire mind, body, and spirit instantly prepare to react to the challenge or threat. The goal of Step 2 is to notice the very real changes that are happening in our mind, body, and spirit. These changes can act like a warning that we are about to lose control to our instincts. Noticing them is our chance to step back from the edge and maintain our power.

When we're challenged or feel threatened, tension can totally fill all parts of ourselves – mind, body, and spirit – so much so, that we can get tunnel vision and become blind to our choices. We can usually feel this in our minds as we become enraged, feel disappointed, or obsessively focused on a perceived wrong. We can feel it in our body when our backs and shoulders tighten, our fists and jaws clench, and our posture becomes upright and rigid. When our mind and our body react in this way, our spirit - our persona, our best self - fades quickly. If we react poorly or inappropriately in this state we can cause a lot of damage to our relationships, reputations, social standing, and overall well-being.

The changes we experience when the fight-flight-freeze response starts are very real. The adrenal glands, in preparation to run or fight, release hormones including adrenaline, norepinephrine, and cortisol. These hormones trigger many physiological (bodily) responses including increased heart rate and blood pressure; rapid breathing and dilated pupils; flushed face from blood moving to muscles, brain, legs, and arms; and possibly even trembling from muscles preparing for action.

This physical reaction is why a lot of people freak out when they feel threatened. To make matters more challenging, it can take up to a whole hour for the body to get rid of these hormones and get back to normal! These physiological reactions can be a good way to identify what is happening, though. If you can notice them, you will know that your body is having a Defense Cascade response. This can be a really helpful tool for taking control of our reactions.

Dr. Robert Plutchik of the University of Washington has identified 6 basic emotions: sadness, happiness, fear, anger, surprise, and disgust. According to Dr. Plutchik, these emotions can be described as follows: Sadness feels like disappointment, grief, or hopelessness. Happiness feels like joy, contentment, and satisfaction. Anger feels like hostility and frustration. Surprises can be good or bad, and it feels like something unexpected. Lastly, Dr. Plutchik states fear is a primal emotion that is important for our survival and can trigger the Defense Cascade.

Being able to identify and categorize your own feelings within this framework can help you understand how you react to different situations. Eventually, you will be able to figure out why these emotions are triggered for you in certain situations. Understanding how you react to these emotions will help you understand your responses to different situations. When feeling anger, disgust, negative surprise, or fear it is extra important to understand your reactions. Understanding what emotions you are experiencing will help you get between the Defense Cascade and your best self, so you can keep your cool.

Start thinking about how your mind, body, and spirit react when your Defense Cascade is engaged. There is an activity at the end of the chapter for you to explore this further. You need to know how you specifically respond, since we are all different. You need to know what your own individual and unique responses are, so that you can keep a lookout for them. This activity will help you better understand your own reactions, so you can tell when your Defense Cascade is engaging.

What are some non-physical threats that could trigger any of our Defense Cascade responses? Not surprisingly, interpersonal rejections are some of the most difficult events in our lives. We do feel real pain when we feel rejected, slighted or have our core beliefs attacked. Sometimes these are real and intentional, other times they are perceived, but that does not matter to the Defense Cascade. Responding to them like a physical threat can deeply effect our relationships, with others and with ourselves, in ways that are not healthy or helpful.

Hurt feelings, jealousy, loneliness, shame, guilt, social anxiety, and embarrassment can all cause our Defense Cascade to be activated when threatened, called-out, challenged, or judged. In the study, "Emotional responses to interpersonal rejection," the authors found that once emotions are set off, our mind and body immediately begin to respond to the perceived threat or opportunity. Think about how quickly you become happy or sad when presented with a positive or negative surprise. This is especially true with the knee-jerk reaction we can have when we are feeling attacked and defensive. If we want to always respond with our best self, we need to gain control over these automatic responses.

Lee and I were reflecting on situations in our high school experiences when there was someone pushing our buttons and we reacted...poorly. This gave the instigators the power to make us react at their whim. Unsurprisingly, once somebody realizes they have the power to get a rise out of person they like to use it. Our problems usually would resolve more quickly, and occur less often, when we remain calm.

You would never want to make an important decision when your Defense Cascade is engaged, but sometimes that is exactly what we do. How many of us have made profound mistakes because we were not not really thinking in difficult moments that have led to very serious consequences? How many times have you later regretted what you have said or done in anger?

Okay, let's get back to what to do in Step 2! You are mad, hurt, disappointed, and/or threatened and your mind, body, and spirit are reacting. In this step, all we need to do is notice that we are reacting. Notice how at this moment, this wrong seems to be all that matters in the entire world. In fact, it is most likely fleeting and will pass in due time. Despite that, our entire self feels threatened. Stop and take full notice of what your body is doing and what your are feeling emotionally. Notice how your anger tries to overtake your mind and body. This can happen whether or not the anger is founded on something truly important. If we allow ourselves to react this way every time we are challenged - and some of us do - we will not have success building interpersonal or professional relationships.

We must notice the changes to our mind, body, and spirit. If we are able to notice how our mind gets hazy and overwhelmed with emotion, how our body gets tight and tense, how our real selves fade into the background, we can take action to stop it.

Again, this generally takes a lot of time and practice to get good at. (Just like learning to tie your shoes or play an instrument!) We also know from experience that this is easier said than done. It is difficult to give yourself time to stop, think, and recognize that the Defense Cascade is taking over while you are being threatened. It can be done though. Step 3 gives us the tool we need to pull it off.

Remember in Step 1, we want to realize that we feel threatened. In Step 2, we want to notice the reaction of our Mind, Body, and Spirit to feeling threatened. Both of these steps prepare us to take action and regain control from the Defense Cascade.

Think of it as:

Step 1: "Yeah, I realize I am challenged or threatened" or "I am angry."

Step 2: "I notice my mind, body, and spirit reacting to being challenged or threatened."

In time, Step 1 and Step 2 will work together as a huge warning that the crap is about to hit the fan. This warning is what will allow you to consciously stop and collect yourself, instead of freaking out. It is important to know that your reaction to any situation is ultimately up to you.

*Surround yourself with positive people
who want you to be your very best.*

END QUESTIONS FOR CHAPTER 4

1. How does our mind, body, and spirit react when the Defense Cascade begins to engage?

_____

_____

2. How does interpersonal rejection cause our Defense Cascade to engage

_____

_____

3. What are the six emotions Dr. Plutnick identifies and how does he describe each of them?

Emotion #1: _____

Emotion #2: _____

Emotion #3: _____

Emotion #4: _____

Emotion #5: _____

Emotion #6: _____

CHAPTER 4 QUOTE QUESTIONS

Danzae Pace is an author and life coach. She writes about the importance of remaining positive and letting difficult moments go.

> "Stress is the trash of modern life – we all generate it,
> but if you don't dispose of it properly,
> it will pile up and overtake your life."
>
> — Danzae Pace

1. What do you think Danzae Pace means by, stress is the trash of modern life?

_____

_____

2. What are some of the bigger stresses in your life?

_____

_____

3. What do you do to relieve stress?

_____

_____

4. Do you think your current coping strategies are effective? Why or why not?

_____

_____

How Your Mind, Body and Spirit React to Emotions

Using Professor Plutchik's list of six basic emotions plus two of your own, list 1-3 words describing how your mind, body, and spirit react and/or feel when you are experiencing the emotion.

LET IT GO
Activity #2

	MIND	BODY	SPIRIT
HAPPINESS			
SADNESS			
ANGER			
FEAR			
Surprise POSITIVE			
Surprise NEGATIVE			
DISGUST			
_____ **Personal #1**			
_____ **Personal #2**			

REACTING TO EMOTIONS
LET IT GO: Activity #2 Continued

When I begin to feel my Defense Cascade engage, what am I going to say to myself in order to recognize I am being triggered?

What do I look like when my Defense Cascade is engaging?

What are my biggest triggers? Why?

Do I use the Defense Cascade too much to deal with daily drama?

How does it feel when your Defense Cascade is engaged?

HOW ATHLETES CAN OVERCOME THE DEFENSE CASCADE

August 1, 2023 | 3andB.com Staff Blog Post
FOR IMMEDIATE RELEASE

Two minutes left in the game. Your team's down by one. The ball comes to you, but–uh oh!–suddenly everything is moving so fast, your heart rate is pounding, and your body just is not responding like it's supposed to. What the heck is going on?

Well, those are common side effects of the Defense Cascade. In stressful situations, our bodies are designed to fight, flee, or sometimes even freeze. For athletes, managing these emotions can be the difference between making the game-winning shot or falling flat on your face.

But fear not because we're going to check out how you can overcome the Defense Cascade to make sure you're prepared for those nerve-racking, in-game moments!

Controlling the Breath

As an athlete, you want to operate at the highest level possible. The problem is that your body's natural response to stress and fear is an increased heart rate and shallow breathing. These symptoms will negatively impact your cardiovascular endurance, create muscle tension, and intensify feelings of panic–that's not going to lead to optimal performance!

So, what can you do?

Take a nice deep breath. Getting control over your breathing will slow the heart rate down, reduce muscle tension, and allow the mind to focus on the job at hand. It is why so many professional basketball players take a few deep breaths before shooting from the free-throw line. As you steady your breathing, your nerves will begin to settle, and you can perform at your all-time best.

Replicating Stress-Inducing Scenarios

No matter how hard you train, the emotions during an actual game will be far higher than during practice. Why? Well, there's simply more on the line. A roaring crowd, the fear of losing, and trash-talk from opponents are enough to send anyone's fight-or-flight response into overdrive!

Simulating high-pressure scenarios is an excellent way to manage your emotions when it is time to perform. In practice, players and teams can do drills that replicate these moments; we call this situational drilling. Adding consequences, such as making the losing team do sprints, intensifies the experience and prepares you for how it will really feel in the game.

Positive Visualization and Self-Talk

The moment that fear and doubt start to kick in can send your thoughts into a downward spiral. Suddenly your mind focuses on worst-case scenarios, and you tell yourself I cannot do this. Our brains are powerful tools, but–boy oh boy–they can also be self-destructive weapons.

You can to take control of your thoughts. Positive visualization and self-talk flip the script in times of stress. Tell yourself that you can do it and that you trained for this very moment. Visualize yourself executing the task perfectly and celebrating at the end of the game.

The more you convince yourself that you can handle the job, the more likely you will be right!

Recognizing Triggers

Whether you like it or not, feeling stress and anxiety is a part of playing sports. Instead of letting the Defense Cascade take you by surprise, learn what triggers your fight-or-flight response and mentally prepare for it. You can do this by thinking about in-game scenarios and past experiences. Make a note of what situations, people, and locations conjure up uneasy emotions.

Knowing your triggers will help you keep a level head when game time rolls around. As soon as one of the stressors manifests, you can immediately identify it and implement coping mechanisms. Not being caught off guard by emotions and having a game plan for when they do occur will do wonders for your overall performance.

Final Thoughts

The Defense Cascade does not have to work against you. In fact, you can use it to your advantage by turning thoughtless reactions into positive behaviors. Recognizing your triggers, using breathing techniques, preparing for in-game scenarios, and filling your head with positivity will all lead to you thriving in high-stake moments and making that game-winning shot.

DEFENSE CASCADE ARTICLE QUESTIONS

1. How does breathing help athletes take control of their Defense Cascade?

_____

_____

2. What specific techniques does the article discuss for helping athletes overcome the Defense Cascade? How does each work?

_____

_____

3. How does knowing their triggers allow athletes to keep a level head during a game?

_____

_____

4. Are you an athlete? If so, have you used any of these techniques before? Did they work for you? Why or why not?

_____

_____

5. If you are not an athlete, how could you use these techniques to improve your life?

_____

_____

DEFINE AND DESCRIBE

Adrenal Glands: _____

_____

Interpersonal rejection: _____

_____

Professional Relationships: _____

_____

Triggers: _____

_____

Positive visualization: _____

_____

Positive self-talk: _____

_____

ADDITIONAL ACTIVITIES

Check out the 3andB.com website for this chapter, just scan the QR code for instant access! Our website contains more information about everything we are discussing, including templates to complete all the work!

CHAPTER 4 ONLINE RESOURCES

SCAN & GO!

Chapter V: Step 3 - Breathe

Objective: The objective of Step 3 is to learn the power of breathing and its effect on mental and physical well-being. By practicing purposeful deep breathing techniques, students can manage stress and anxiety, improve focus, process information more effectively, and make better decisions..

Chapter 5 Overview

- Breathing is a key tool to manage the Defense Cascade and regain control in difficult situations.
- Taking a purposeful deep breath in through the nose, holding it for a moment, and then exhaling slowly through the mouth can stop the fight-flight-freeze response.
- Breathing is also important for mental and spiritual well-being and can reduce stress and anxiety.
- The 3andB Breathing Technique involves deep breathing and focusing on different parts of the body to relax the mind, body, and spirit.
- Being calm and present in difficult situations allows for better processing of information and more effective solutions.

Video and Audio Resources

https://3andb.com/let-it-go-high-school-chapter-5-step-3-breathe/

Chapter 5 Video Introduction
Chapter 5 Audio and Article Audio

Readings & Activities:
1. Starter Activity
2. Chapter 5 Text
3. Chapter 5 End Questions
4. Chapter 5 Quote Questions
5. Chapter 5 Article
6. Chapter 5 Article Questions & Vocabulary
7. More Resources

CHAPTER 5 ONLINE
RESOURCES

SCAN & GO!

CHAPTER 5 STARTER ACTIVITY: STEP 3 - BREATHE

In Chapter 5, we discover the vital role breathing plays in reclaiming control from the Defense Cascade. Breathing is our ultimate weapon for restoring our true selves when the Fight-Flight-Freeze response kicks in. Breathing is a lifelong tool that empowers us to remain calm, composed, and collected in any situation. By simply taking a deep breath, we signal to our Mind, Body, and Spirit that we're ready to tackle challenges with our best self, leaving the Defense Cascade behind.

Continuously develop your Mind, Body, & Spirit to live your best life!

Check the box that best applies to you!

☐ **I HAVE** used breathing techniques to deal with difficult moments.

☐ **I HAVE NOT** used breathing techniques to deal with difficult moments.

Take a quiet moment for yourself. Take a deep breath in through your nose and let it fill your entire chest and belly with air. Hold it for a moment, then exhale. How do you feel?

_____

_____

_____

In the past, how have you dealt with your emotions after you were upset or angry? Do you have an activity to help you manage your emotions?

_____

_____

_____

In our hectic lives, it's easy to overlook the small wonders that bring us joy and fulfillment. But by embracing gratitude, we open our eyes to the abundance of good in our daily lives. Before exploring Step 3, take a moment to recognize and appreciate the people, places, and things that inspire gratitude within you today.

I AM GRATEFUL FOR THIS PERSON:	I AM GRATEFUL FOR THIS TEACHER:	I AM GRATEFUL FOR THIS FRIEND:
_____	_____	_____

I AM GRATEFUL FOR THIS PLACE:	I AM GRATEFUL FOR THIS OPPORTUNITY:	I AM GRATEFUL FOR THIS THING:
_____	_____	_____

"Breath is the bridge
which connects life
to consciousness,
which unites your body
to your thoughts."

— Thich Nhat Hanh

Chapter V

Step 3: Breathe

Now that we are beginning to realize and notice how our Defense Cascade affects us when we are feeling threatened, we need to get in-between the threat and the activation so our best self can respond appropriately. We can do this by simply breathing.

When our flight-flight-freeze response is activated our breathes become shorter, our heart rate increases so we are ready to run or fight. This is all automatic. We can stop the fight-flight-freeze response by taking a purposeful deep breath in through the nose (if possible), holding it for a moment, and then exhaling slowly through the mouth. This deep breath communicates to ourselves that we are okay and not in imminent danger. It is a great way to signal to ourselves that we are choosing to use our best self to think through the situation, instead of just reacting to it.

When you realize and notice that your Defense Cascade is activating - breathe. Take a long deep breath and, if it is safe, close your eyes for a moment, then exhale. Take another deep breath, give yourself time, and exhale. Repeat this cycle, breathing in deeply and exhaling as we allow ourselves the time and space for our rational mind and best self to reemerge.

In "Understanding the Defense Cascade" from the Harvard Review of Psychiatry, the authors discuss how animals are able to return to a normal state of functioning relatively quickly once a threat is removed. Unfortunately, they also note, humans often struggle to return to a normal state. This is sometimes the case even after a long period of time has passed. Breathing is the key for humans to return to a normal state once the Defense Cascade has been activated.

Breathing is so important, not only to our body, but also to our mental and spiritual well-being. We cannot stress enough the importance of learning a really good breathing technique for the best management of your Mind, Body, and Spirit in all areas of your life.

Two separate studies from the Journal of American College Health concluded that learning breathing techniques to reduce stress and induce calm are extremely effective. The studies concluded that breathing techniques provided long-lasting stress and anxiety reduction to those who continued to use breathing techniques in all aspects of their lives.

So, the secret here is to master breathing. Breathing is the key to taking back control of, not only the Defense Cascade, but many aspects of your life. Even in happy moments, learn to take a deep breath to take in and completely enjoy the moment. Breathing makes us present. Breathing is one of the keys to living our best life.

If we are able to realize when we feel threatened, are able to notice how our entire self is reacting, and then stop to breathe, we can get in between our automatic Defense Cascade and our best self. Breathing is the key that unlocks the power to control the Defense Cascade. This is something we can achieve anytime, anywhere!

Even in more difficult situations that we cannot let go of immediately, breathing will assist you in regaining control and focus. Making quick decisions in a defensive state can be a recipe for making the situation worse. Maybe way worse. Taking a deep breath and allowing yourself to take a moment, even just a few seconds, to regain control in a difficult situation can make all the difference.

Your activity for Step 3 is to simply get breathing. We have developed a very simple step-by-step breathing technique from our own research and experience. Give our technique a try and explore the many others that are available. Find what works best for you. Now that you know the importance of breathing, give yourself some time to breathe purposefully.

Let's give it a try.

3andB Breathing Technique

Breathe in through your nose, letting your lungs and belly fill completely with air.

As you breathe in, focus on the air filling your lungs and belly. Allow the air to fill your being completely.

As you take a deep breath, take notice of the air filling your entire being as your mind starts to become clear. Your emotions become calmer, and you are now more in control of yourself. Now exhale. (Calming of the mind)

As you take a deep breath, take notice of the air filling your entire being. Feel the air flow into you and consciously move your awareness throughout your body. As you slowly shift your awareness, allow that part of your body to loosen and relax. Feel the loosening of your neck, shoulders, and back. Allow the air to fill your torso and work its way through your arms, hands, and fingers. Keep breathing as the air continues down into your hips, legs, and feet. Repeat this as necessary. Cycle through the different parts of your body until they are all loose and relaxed. Now exhale. (Calming of the body)

As you take a deep breath, take notice of the air filling your entire being. Breathe in order to allow your mind to clear, your spirit to return and your best self to re-emerge. You are now ready to put proper perspective on the moment. Now exhale. (Calming of the spirit)

As your mind, body, and spirit relax, you regain more of yourself. Your best self emerges.

Contiue to breath, exhaling through your nose, and allow your entire Mind, Body, and Spirit to relax.

If possible and safe, close your eyes through this process. Focus on returning your Mind, Body, and Spirit to your best self.

Repeat until your mind is calm, your body is cool, your spirit is collected, and your best self has returned.

You are now present and ready to deal with the situation as your best self.

When you practice this breathing technique on your own, become mindful of how your Mind, Body, and Spirit react. Being able to be calm and collected in any situation is a real superpower and - breathing is the key to unlocking it.

Being calm in the face of confrontation is a very important life skill. We always want to be our best when dealing with life's problems. When we are fully present it allows us to remain in control, process information better and develop more effective solutions.

Once you are in a difficult situation, start your breathing technique to get control over the Defense Cascade. Breathe for as long as the situation will allow. The more time you take for yourself, the better. Even a few more seconds spent breathing before you respond can significantly increase the quality of your response. This might look like just walking away, dropping it entirely, or coming back to it later once you've had time to process everything. Learning to breathe in these difficult moments is about us becoming present and taking back control of the situation.

As we realize that our Mind, Body, and Spirit are filled with emotions when threatened, and with our new breathing technique in hand, we can now allow ourselves a moment to let go of the emotions and regain complete control of our senses. Once we are more in control of ourselves and our thinking mind is back with us, then we can make our next move. It will surely be wiser!

Again, this is easier said than done and it certainly takes practice. Once you start putting these steps into practice each and every day, you will create a new behavior to support yourself. Instead of reacting quickly and blindly, you will breathe, take a moment for yourself, become present, and regain composure and perspective. Over time, you will learn how to use breathing to remain present and to respond as your best self in all situations.

That is all Step 3 is about, taking taking back self-control through breathing. You can use breathing techniques in all areas of your life to remain present and live life completely.

Let's review where we are in the seven-step process.

Step 1 is to realize that we have been challenged or threatened which begins to activate our Defense Cascade.

Step 2 is to notice how our Mind, Body, and Spirit are reacting to the Defense Cascade being engaged.

Step 3 is to breathe in order to get in-between the threat and the Defense Cascade so we can regain control and allow our best self to reemerge. We use breathing to regain control from the Defense Cascade after we realize the cascade has been triggered (Step1) and we notice the warning signs (Step 2).

In Step 4 we will begin to learn a little bit more about ourselves and our reactions to problematic situations.

Learn to breathe to regain control and be your best self.

END QUESTIONS FOR CHAPTER 5

1. What is the purpose of breathing in the 7-step Let It Go process?

_____

_____

2. What does taking a deep breath in a difficult situation communicate to your mind, body, and spirit?

_____

_____

3. How many times should you take a deep breath before responding when you feel your Defense Cascade engaging?

_____

_____

4. When is it a good idea to close your eyes while using a breathing technique?

_____

_____

5. Beyond the breathing for the Let It Go process, how can breathing benefit you in your everyday life?

_____

_____

CHAPTER 5 QUOTE QUESTIONS

Thich Nhat Nanh was a teacher, writer and Vietnamese Buddhist monk. He is credited with being the father of "mindfulness." Dr. Martin Luther King, Jr. nominated him for the Nobel Peace Prize in January 1967. Dr. Marting Luther King, Jr. named Thich Nhat Nanh "an apostle of peace and nonviolence." He strongly encouraged his followers to use breathing as a means to better understand themselves.

> "Breath is the bridge which connects life to consciousness, which unites your body to your thoughts."
>
> — Thich Nhat Hanh

1. Doing a search for Thich Nhat Nanh, what are three things you find interesting or compelling about his life?

_____

_____

_____

2. Why did Dr. Martin Luther King, Jr. nominate Thich Nhat Hanh for the Nobel Peace Prize?

_____

_____

3. Why do you think Thich Nhat Nanh values breathing?

_____

_____

Breathing to Restore our Best Self
or
Simplified Breathing Technique

Take 15-20 minutes to practice using the 3andB Simplified Breathing Technique or as we like to call it, Breathing to Restore Our Best Self.
Do 3 sessions of 5-7 minutes each. After each session describe how you feel.

LET IT GO
Activity #3

3andB Breathing Technique

1 Breathe in through your nose, letting your lungs and belly fill completely with air.

2 As you breathe in, focus on the air filling your lungs and belly. Allow the air to fill your being completely.

3 As you take a deep breath, take notice of the air filling your entire being as your mind starts to become clear. Your emotions become calmer, and you are now more in control of yourself. Exhale. (*Calming of the mind*)

4 As you take a deep breath, take notice of the air filling your entire being. Feel the air working its way throughout your body. Feel the loosening of your neck, shoulders, and back. Allow the air to fill your torso and work its way through your arms, hands, and fingers. Keep breathing as the air continues down into your hips, legs, and feet. Exhale. (*Calming of the body*)

5 As you take a deep breath, take notice of the air filling your entire being. Allow your mind to clear, your spirit to return and your best self to re-emerge. You are now ready to put proper perspective on the moment. Exhale. (*Calming of the spirit*)

6 As your mind, body, and spirit relax, you regain more of yourself. Your best self emerges.

7 Exhale through your nose, and allow your entire Mind, Body, and Spirit to relax.

8 If possible and safe, close your eyes through this process. Focus on returning your Mind, Body, and Spirit to your best self.

9 Repeat until your mind is calm, your body is cool, your spirit is collected, and your best self has returned.

10 You are now present and ready to deal with the situation as your best self.

Breathing Session 1: How did you feel after session 1?

Breathing Session 2: How did you feel after session 2?

Breathing Session 3: How did you feel after session 3?

ACTORS AND MUSICIANS USE BREATHING TECHNIQUES TO PERFORM AT THEIR VERY BEST

August 1, 2023 | 3andB.com Staff Blog Post
FOR IMMEDIATE RELEASE

Actors, actresses and musicians spend countless hours perfecting their crafts and developing the skills necessary to deliver outstanding performances. One of the most critical skills these professionals use is proper breathing techniques. These are important tools that allow them to remain calm and present, enabling them to perform at their maximum potential.

Breathing Techniques for Actors and Actresses

Breathing techniques are essential for actors and actresses to create and maintain the proper tone and inflection while delivering their lines. These practices also help them control their emotions, which not only helps them stay in character but also really helps to control nerves and anxiety. This is particularly important in high-pressure situations, such as auditions or live performances, where one mistake could make all the difference.

One of the most common breathing techniques used by actors and actresses is deep breathing. This involves taking long, slow breaths in through the nose and out through the mouth. By focusing on their breath, actors and actresses can slow their heart rates, calm their nerves, and stay in control.

Another technique used by actors and actresses is visualization. This involves imagining a calming scenario or image in their minds, such as a peaceful beach or a beautiful sunset. Focusing on this image allows them to reduce stress and remain calm, even in the most high-intensity situations.

Breathing Techniques for Musicians

Musicians, especially singers and instrumentalists use breathing techniques to achieve greater control and precision in their performances. Singers rely on proper breathing techniques to hit high notes and maintain their vocal range. On the other hand, instrumentalists use breathing to control their phrasing, dynamics, and timing.

One technique used by singers is the lip trill. This involves making a buzzing sound with their lips while exhaling, which helps them warm up their vocal cords and develop better breath control. Singers also use breathing exercises such as inhaling for a set amount of time and exhaling for a longer time to improve their lung capacity.

Alternatively, instrumentalists use breathing techniques to control the sound of their instruments. For example, brass and woodwind players use their breath to create vibrato and dynamics. Through breath control, they can produce a wide range of sounds and achieve greater control over their performances.

Other Practices for Maintaining Professional Levels of Performance

In addition to proper breathing techniques, actors, actresses, and musicians also prioritize their overall well-being to maintain their professional level of performance. This includes engaging in regular exercise, maintaining a healthy diet, and getting enough sleep. However, many even take it a step further and avoid using substances such as tobacco and alcohol, which can have a negative impact on their performances.

The truth is that data has consistently shown that regular exercise is essential for maintaining physical and mental health. It can help to reduce stress and anxiety, increase energy levels, and improve overall well-being. Eating a healthy diet is also essential as it provides the necessary nutrients and energy to fuel any kind of performance. Finally, getting enough sleep is critical for allowing the body and mind to rest and recharge, ensuring performers are alert and focused when it counts.

What High School Students Can Learn from Actors and Musicians

High school students can learn a lot from actors and musicians about using breathing techniques to perform at their best. They can also adopt other practices, such as regular exercise, a healthy diet, and getting enough sleep, to maintain their energy levels and stay focused throughout the day.

Either way, breathing techniques can be especially helpful for students during stressful situations, such as exams, speeches, or performances. By taking deep, slow breaths, they can calm their nerves and stay focused on the task at hand.

Closing Thoughts

Breathing techniques are crucial for the success of actors, actresses, and musicians, allowing them to remain calm, control their emotions, and perform at their maximum potential. High school students can benefit from adopting these techniques and other practices such as exercise, healthy eating, and getting enough sleep to reduce stress and improve focus. By following the example of performers, students can learn to perform at their best in academic and extracurricular activities.

BREATHING ARTICLE QUESTIONS

1. Why is breathing an important skill for musicians, actors, and actresses to deliver their best performances?

_____

_____

2. How does deep breathing help actors and actresses deliver an amazing performance?

_____

_____

3. How does regular exercise help musicians, actors, and actresses deliver outstanding performances?

_____

_____

4. If you are an actor/actress or musician, how can you incorporate breathing into your performances?

_____

_____

5.How can you incorporate breathing techniques to improve your life?

_____

_____

DEFINE AND DESCRIBE

Consciousness: _____

_____

Mindfulness: _____

_____

Deep Breathing: _____

_____

Calm: _____

_____

Positive Mindset: _____

_____

Stress: _____

_____

ADDITIONAL ACTIVITIES

Check out the 3andB.com website for this chapter, just scan the QR code for instant access! Our website contains more information about everything we are discussing, including templates to complete all the work!

CHAPTER 5 ONLINE RESOURCES

SCAN & GO!

Chapter VI: Step 4 - Engage Introspection

Objective: The objective of Step 4 is to have students develop a deeper understanding of self-reflection and its benefits in identifying personal beliefs and fears that drive defensive reactions. They will recognize the impact of self-awareness with their social connections, job performances and overall happiness. Students will learn effective strategies to improve their self-awareness through asking themselves pertinent questions, recognizing the importance of not sweating the small stuff and understanding others' perspectives.

Chapter 6 Overview

• Step 4 of the Let It Go process encourages self-reflection to understand the reasons behind defensive reactions when faced with a challenge.
• 85-90% of people lack adequate self-awareness, leading to issues in social connections, job performances and happiness.
• Self-reflection helps identify personal beliefs and fears, which can aid individuals in understanding why they react a certain way to certain challenges.
• Asking oneself questions about core beliefs and passions can help gain insight into one's own values, while also allowing for better understanding of others' perspectives.
• Remembering to not sweat the small stuff is important for true self-understanding and growth.

Video and Audio Resources

https://3andb.com/let-it-go-high-school-chapter-6-step-4-engage-introspection/

Chapter 6 Video Introduction
Chapter 6 Audio and Article Audio

CHAPTER 6 ONLINE RESOURCES

SCAN & GO!

Readings & Activities:
1. Starter Activity
2. Chapter 6 Text
3. Chapter 6 End Questions
4. Chapter 6 Quote Questions
5. Chapter 6 Article
6. Chapter 6 Article Questions & Vocabulary
7. More Resources

CHAPTER 6 STARTER ACTIVITY: STEP 4 - ENGAGE INTROSPECTION

In Chapter 6, we learn more about the importance of being self-aware and understanding who we are as a person. Being self-aware means having a conscious understanding of one's own character, feelings, motivations, and desires. It involves recognizing one's strengths and weaknesses, as well as the thoughts and emotions that influence their behavior. With this understanding, people can gain insight into who they are as individuals and how they fit into the world around them.

Continuously develop your Mind, Body, & Spirit to live your best life!

What is self-awareness? How well do you know yourself?

_____

_____

What are some of your strengths and weaknesses?

_____

_____

What type of person do you want to be as you approach graduation?

_____

_____

_____

In our hectic lives, it's easy to overlook the small wonders that bring us joy and fulfillment. But by embracing gratitude, we open our eyes to the abundance of good in our daily lives. Before exploring Step 4, take a moment to recognize and appreciate the people, places, and things that inspire gratitude within you today.

I AM GRATEFUL FOR THIS PERSON:	I AM GRATEFUL FOR THIS TEACHER:	I AM GRATEFUL FOR THIS FRIEND:

I AM GRATEFUL FOR THIS PLACE:	I AM GRATEFUL FOR THIS OPPORTUNITY:	I AM GRATEFUL FOR THIS THING:

"Who looks outside, dreams;
who looks inside, awakes."

— Carl Jung

Chapter VI

Step 4: Engage Introspection

It is time to turn our gaze inwards and learn more about ourselves. Step 4 is not only meant to be used as part of the Let It Go process, but something to be used each day of our lives. Step 4 is all about being introspective, or turning our attention inwards and being honest with ourselves. As Socrates once said, "Know thyself!"

We need to understand why we react defensively in situations where it is not necessary or helpful. In order to change our reactions, we need to understand our own views about ourselves, others and the world in general. It is when our strongly held beliefs are challenged that we feel the need to defend ourselves and get angry, mad, sad, upset, etc. Once we better understand our own inner beliefs, we will better understand why we are triggered when someone challenges or threatens them.

Reflecting on our own selves can be difficult. We need to be honest with ourselves, and sometimes this can be tough. For some of us, getting professional assistance can make this process much easier. If you have beliefs or trauma that are very difficult for you to think about or overcome, we highly encourage you to reach out for some extra help. Please contact a trusted adult such as a family member, school counselor, or teacher. They can help you with resources and next steps. We all need professional help sometimes, and the professionals know how to best support us during difficult situations. Always get professional help when anything you are dealing with feels too overwhelming.

Many of our viewpoints started really early in our lives. Our beliefs are developed through our direct experiences, both good and bad. Our points of view are what we use to determine what is and is not good for us. They are the framework for our decision making processes. For the most part, they serve us well each day. Sometimes, though, when these deeply held beliefs are challenged, we feel like we need to defend them.

According to Tasha Eurich, a leading organizational psychologist with the Harvard Business Review, research has shown that 95% of people believe that they are self-aware. In actuality, only 10-15% of people really are aware of themselves and the impacts their actions have on others. Studies have shown that people who are not self-aware cut the chances of a team's success by more than half. It is common for non-self-aware people to have difficulties making social connections, which can create problems when working in groups or teams.

This means 85-90% of us are walking around without a clear idea of who we are and how we are viewed by others. This is potentially a huge problem. Self-awareness is important for healthy interpersonal relationships, quality job performance, and successful careers. In fact, and maybe most importantly, it helps us simply be happy within ourselves. Individuals who are not self-aware have a hard time accepting criticism, understanding the perspective of others, and communicating with others. They often hurt others' feelings without being aware of it and frequently blame failures on everybody but themselves.

Each of us can do better by becoming more self-aware.

We all want to be loved and treated with respect. In the previously mentioned study, "Emotional Responses to Interpersonal Rejection," the article discusses how important being accepted by our family, friends, and co-workers is to most of us. It turns out that being accepted by our family and peers is extremely important. We are social creatures and we want to feel as though we are valued among our community. When we feel our value to the community is being questioned, we view it as a threat to our security within that community. This could activate our Defense Cascade. Becoming more self-aware will allow us to be more confident in ourselves, find more acceptance from others, and increase our resilience.

It is very important that we feel accepted and part of a community that cares about us. As social creatures, we are highly attuned to possible rejection. When we are super reactive and defensive, it can make it harder to feel accepted. It also makes it harder for others to accept us!

Imagine for a second that you hear that somebody called you a liar. Your first reaction might be to freak out (that is the Defense Cascade talking!). In our society, lying has serious consequences to our social standing. It makes sense that it would be upsetting to be called a liar, but if we know we did not lie that allows us to have a foundation to explore the situation without freaking out. Thinking about why somebody might view you that way can give some insight into why they might have said that. If you know what your point of view is, you can try looking at a situation from somebody else's viewpoint and that makes talking out the problem way easier.

Learning about who we are and what we believe can be a real challenge for many of us. It can be really daunting to pull apart and analyze our beliefs honestly so we can fully understand their true nature. In the article, "Know Thy Selves: Learning to Understand Oneself Increases the Ability to Understand Others," the authors concluded that knowing yourself well allows you to put yourself in somebody else's shoes so that you can better understand their perspective. Subjects in the study practiced perspective-taking skills for 3-months and at the end of the study they were much more effective at dealing with interpersonal problems. This was because they understood how their own beliefs affected the problem.

When our beliefs and the beliefs of others are different, when they interact there can be conflicts. So what are your beliefs? We have attached a worksheet for you to explore with yourself! The most important part of this worksheet is honesty. Have fun, be open, and allow for self-exploration.

Learning about who we are by asking questions about ourselves is very important. Asking ourselves questions like: What are some misconceptions I have about myself and the world around me? How do other people perceive me? How would I like them to perceive me? What do I love doing? What are my passions? What impact do I want to make? What are my core beliefs that drive my decisions and are they correct and true? These types of questions can lead to genuine understanding as to why we react the way we do in many circumstances.

Again, for most of us, we can ask ourselves these questions and work through to find the hard answers. If you have dealt with difficult situations and trauma, you may need professional help working through these questions and answers.

If you answer these questions honestly, by the end, you should have a better understanding of what you love, what you are passionate about, your beliefs, and your fears. Reflect on why your beliefs are so meaningful to you. Never be afraid to ask yourself if your beliefs are correct and accurate. Question everything.

There are many ideas that were once widely accepted that turned out to be wrong, like flat wrong. For a long time, we believed the Earth was flat. It is not. As you know, it is very round. Spontaneous generation of life was another one from way back when. Yes, they thought that life forms could appear from nothing. Maggots born from raw meat? Nope, humans at the time weren't aware of the life cycle of insects. Original estimates of the age of the planet Earth made the planet 50 times younger than reality. DNA was first theorized to contain three strands. There are only two. The universe was originally thought to have always existed. It was called the "steady state" model, but the big-bang changed all that. Now with the launching of the new James Webb space telescope, even the big bang is being questioned. Einstein got the universe wrong when he called it "constant", which he later recognized as his "greatest blunder." How can we forget the geocentric theory? You know, the Earth being in the center of the universe. We could go on and on.

All of those theories were wrong, but at the time, they believed they were undeniably right. So before you go fighting the good fight over something you believe so strongly to be correct, think about some of these examples. Even the brightest minds don't get it right all the time. Think back to your time in elementary school. How much has changed since then? The point is, reflect on your strongly held beliefs and ask yourself if they will still be true in a few days, weeks, or years. Will your strongly held beliefs stand the test of time? Are those beliefs worth the effort and conviction? Sometimes they are and sometimes they aren't.

We are only human, and we all make mistakes. We each have had countless experiences that shape our sense of self and our own unique perspectives. Compare your perspective to the outside world. Are they aligned? A good way to determine this is to observe how often you find yourself in difficult situations with others. The more often you find yourself in difficult situations or conflict, the more often your reality is coming into conflict with outer reality. Yes, of course it happens occasionally, but if it is a constant pattern in your life you likely have some reflecting to do.

Start by regularly reflecting on your beliefs. Keep those that serve and align with your world, and disregard those that cause disruption and conflict in your life. Step back and observe how your internal reality and beliefs intersect with external reality. Knowing how you present yourself to the outer world will increase your chances for successful relationships, both personal and professional.

A truly interesting quote by a very smart old dude states, "The only thing I know for certain is that I know nothing." Plato said this after observing Socrates teach. They both understood that there are no eternal truths, just beliefs that may or may not hold up, given today's current knowledge. As you begin to reflect on your own beliefs, realize they may not be as solid as they feel right now. Will they stand the test of time?

Practice self-reflection daily by asking how do my beliefs serve me? Are my beliefs building a prosperous, peaceful, loving world around me? Or do my beliefs hurt me and those around me? Whatever the answer, we all have some reflecting to do to become more self-aware.

Understanding yourself and your own beliefs will make you better situated to deal with the emotions that arise when your point of view is challenged. Use the attached activity to start learning more about yourself. Then each day, reflect on your beliefs and how well they serve or do not serve you. You can even begin journaling to help keep track of your progress. Ask yourself, does this belief help me life my best life? How does it help me? Explore other methods of learning about yourself and furthering your beliefs as well.

Let's review.

Step 1 is the realization that I feel threatened - mad, upset, hurt, filled with drama.

Step 2 is noticing how your mind, body and spirit react to feeling threatened.

Step 3 is to take a deep breath and get in-between our automatic Defense Cascade and our thinking mind.

Now we add Step 4, where we become increasingly aware of our own beliefs and how our beliefs affect our reactions, especially when those beliefs are challenged. Daily practice of Step 4 can really increase our self-awareness.

Lastly, remember what Einstein said, "When you look at yourself from a universal standpoint, something inside always reminds you that there are bigger and better things to worry about." Don't sweat the small stuff, and most of it is small stuff.

END QUESTIONS FOR CHAPTER 6

1. What do you think Socrates meant when he said "Know thyself!"? What does this mean to you?

_____

_____

2. How does a person's self-awareness affect their relationships? Do you think this is important? Why or why not?

_____

_____

3. Do you frequently find yourself in conflict with yourself or others? If yes or no, why do you think that might be?

_____

_____

4. Why is it important to regularly self-reflect on your own beliefs?

_____

_____

5. What about yourself do you want to learn more about?

_____

_____

CHAPTER 6 QUOTE QUESTIONS

In the following article we will learn more about Carl Jung and his role in the development of modern psychology. Before reading the article, speculate on what you think Carl Jung meant when he said,

“Who looks outside dreams;
who looks inside, awakes?”

.

1. What does Carl Jung mean by “who looks outside dreams?”

_____

_____

2. What does Carl Jung mean by “who looks inside, awakes?”

_____

_____

_____

3. Do you spend more time looking inside or outside?

_____

_____

_____

_____

Look inside and become more self-aware.

Engage Introspection: Becoming More Self-Aware

Begin your self-reflection journey by answering the following questions. Be open and honest with yourself as you explore who you are and how others see you.

LET IT GO
Activity #4

DATE: _____

Am I living up to the potential of my best self and my best life?

Am I using my life and time wisely?

Am I taking anyone or anything in my life for granted?

Am I maintaining a healthy perspective and a positive mindset each day?

Engage Introspection:
Becoming more Self-Aware
LET IT GO: Activity #4

Am I making the most of each and every day?

Am I putting enough effort into maintaining and building my relationships?

Am I taking care of myself mentally, physically, and spiritually?

Am I letting others or matters outside of my control to negatively affect my life?

Are you happy, why or why not?

WHAT IS INTROSPECTION AND WHAT DOES CARL JUNG HAVE TO DO WITH IT?

August 1, 2023 | 3andB.com Staff Blog Post
FOR IMMEDIATE RELEASE

Have you ever wondered why some people seem to be able to live their best life, while others constantly find themselves down in the dumps? Carl Jung had quite an insightful theory on why this occurs, and it all comes down to introspection.

He believed that by simply taking the time to reflect on our thoughts and behaviors, we could identify the areas we need to improve to lead a more fulfilling and successful life. So, if you're looking for ways to finally begin living your best life, it may be time to turn to good old-fashioned introspection!

Who is Carl Jung?

Before we hop headfirst into the topic of introspection, let's take a moment to learn about the man of the hour, Carl Jung. He was a Swiss psychologist and psychiatrist who is most well-known for his part in introducing analytic psychology to the world.

Jung's most notable work focused on introverted and extroverted personalities, the collective unconscious, archetypes, and introspection. Most of his work was done in response to Sigmund Freud, another founding father of psychology who had some impressively accurate… and some not-so-accurate theories and ideas about how our minds work.

Jung worked closely with Freud, finding that his research led him to agree with and confirm many of Freud's hypotheses. That was, until 1912, when their paths diverged. Carl Jung then published Wandlungen und Symbole der Libido (Psychology of the Unconscious), a book directly disputing many of Freud's ideas and theories.

Jung's Findings on Introspection

Once Carl Jung turned away from Freud, he decided to turn his attention to understanding his own fantasies and dreams. Where did they come from? And why did they seem so important to him?

For many years, Jung focused this research on older people, many of which found themselves struggling with feeling empty and like they missed out on living their best life. This is where introspection comes in.

Jung found that every one of his patients had their own individual ideas about what a fulfilling, happy life is. The common thread that he found was that those that looked outside themselves for happiness tended to feel empty and unfulfilled. Money, material things and the approval of others didn't end up giving what they needed. However, those that tended to look within were truly happier. True happiness was found by looking within.

As he has said in the past, "All factors which are generally assumed to make for happiness can, under certain conditions, produce the contrary. No matter how ideal your situation may be, it does not necessarily guarantee happiness."

What Does This Have To Do with Me?

Yes, I know you may find yourself wondering just how relevant Mr. Jung's theories of introspection are to helping you keep your cool. They are more relevant than you might believe.

We are all different! This means different lifestyles make different people happy. Different things cause different people to lose their cool, too. It also means that living YOUR best life is not going to look like your favorite influencer's, or even your best friend's, life!

Jung found that, to truly live your best life, you must look within. Yes, I know that sounds like a cliché, but that is for good reason. While watching your phone light up with notifications, buying into the newest TikTok trend, and getting the approval of your friends might feel great in the moment, that feeling of satisfaction eventually wears off and leaves you feeling empty.

Do you really want to live your best life? Well, to do that, you have to begin looking within you. What makes you feel the most fulfilled? What leaves you feeling on top of the world? Looking inwards and deepening your connection with yourself will give you a strong foundation to build yourself up. This is where you will find true happiness. This is where you will live your best life.

INTROSPECTION ARTICLE QUESTIONS

1. What do you think Carl Jung would suggest you do in order to feel like you had a good life when you are old?

_____

_____

2. Think about 3 people you know pretty well. What makes each of them happy? Are they all the same? Are they the same as what makes you happy?

_____

_____

3. Take a few moments to think about what is really important to you. Describe why it is more important to you than it might be to somebody else.

_____

_____

4. What activities make you feel excited and inspired?

_____

_____

5.How will you incorporate daily introspection into your life?

_____

_____

DEFINE AND DESCRIBE

Introspection: _____

_____

Self-reflection: _____

_____

Self-awareness: _____

_____

Viewpoints: _____

_____

Fulfilled: _____

_____

Contentment: _____

_____

ADDITIONAL ACTIVITIES

Check out the 3andB.com website for this chapter, just scan the QR code for instant access! Our website contains more information about everything we are discussing, including templates to complete all the work!

CHAPTER 6 ONLINE RESOURCES

SCAN & GO!

Chapter VII: Step 5 - Awareness

Objective: Students will be able to increase their self-awareness, understand the benefits of forgiveness and challenge their beliefs to create new perspectives in difficult situations. They will also learn how to maintain a relaxed state of mind, body, and spirit to deal with challenging situations as their best selves. This will lead to increased personal growth, improved relationships, and better mental and emotional health.

Chapter 7 Overview

• Step 5 of the Let It Go process is called Awareness and it involves being able to step back from difficult situations and open ourselves up to new alternatives and perspectives.
• Being aware of possible alternatives in a less-than-ideal situation can help create different reactions to triggers.
• Allowing our beliefs to be challenged is how we grow as a person and it allows for greater understanding and growth.
• Having the self-awareness to realize why a conflict exists will reveal a lot about you. It will also give you a lot to think about and reflect on.
• Forgiveness is another important life-hack that involves forgiving yourself and others to increase health and well-being.
• When we are wrong, we can admit our mistakes and learn from them, and when we are right, we can give the other person the grace to be wrong or just chalk it up to life not always being fair.
• Being in a relaxed state of mind, body, and spirit allows us to deal with the situation at hand as our best selves.

Video and Audio Resources

https://3andb.com/let-it-go-high-school-chapter-7-step-5-awareness/

Chapter 7 Video Introduction
Chapter 7 Audio and Article Audio

Readings & Activities:
1. Starter Activity
2. Chapter 7 Text
3. Chapter 7 End Questions
4. Chapter 7 Quote Questions
5. 16Personalities.Com Worksheets.
6. Chapter 7 Article
7. Chapter 7 Article Questions & Vocabulary
8. More Resources

CHAPTER 7 ONLINE RESOURCES

SCAN & GO!

CHAPTER 7 STARTER ACTIVITY: STEP 5 - AWARENESS

In Chapter 7, we dive into the significance of understanding our own beliefs and perspectives. By doing so, we can approach challenging moments from different angles and gain a deeper understanding of ourselves and others. This self-awareness is crucial when facing difficult situations as it enables us to see things from the other person's point of view. Ultimately, the more we comprehend ourselves, the more effective solutions we can create.

Continuously develop your Mind, Body, & Spirit to live your best life!

Check the box that best applies to you!

☐ **I ALWAYS ADMIT & APOLOGIZE** when I am wrong or hurt someone.

☐ **I DO NOT ALWAYS ADMIT & APOLOGIZE** when I am wrong or hurt someone.

Do you appreciate your views being challenged? Why or why not?

_____

_____

_____

Do you find it easy or hard to forgive others who have wronged or hurt you? Why?

_____

_____

_____

In our hectic lives, it's easy to overlook the small wonders that bring us joy and fulfillment. But by embracing gratitude, we open our eyes to the abundance of good in our daily lives. Before exploring Step 5, take a moment to recognize and appreciate the people, places, and things that inspire gratitude within you today.

I AM GRATEFUL FOR THIS PERSON:	I AM GRATEFUL FOR THIS TEACHER:	I AM GRATEFUL FOR THIS FRIEND:
_____	_____	_____
I AM GRATEFUL FOR THIS PLACE:	**I AM GRATEFUL FOR THIS OPPORTUNITY:**	**I AM GRATEFUL FOR THIS THING:**
_____	_____	_____

"The better awareness,
the better your choices.
As you make better choices,
you will see better results."

— Anonymous

Chapter VII

Step 5: Awareness

Have you ever been really mad at someone over something and it turns out you were completely wrong? It happens. You get mad about something and then when all the facts come together it turns out you were incorrect. Not a great place to be especially if you got angry and overreacted.

You are probably starting to see how these steps work together. Step 1, 2, and 3 work together to help us realize, notice, and stop the Defense Cascade from engaging. Step 4 and Step 5 work together in a similar way to help us create different reactions to our triggers. From Step 4, we are now beginning to understand ourselves better and how we react when our beliefs are challenged. In Step 5 we ask ourselves, "How can we put this moment into perspective?"

If we are able step back from a difficult situation we can open ourselves up to new alternatives, different possibilities, and/or the next best option. Maybe we are wrong. Maybe we do not have all the information. Maybe we might need to accept that sometimes life just isn't fair. Becoming aware of the possible alternatives in a less-than-ideal situation is what Step 5 is about.

Do not be afraid to give yourself some space to find new possibilities! We can do this by allowing our mind to be open to different understandings and new perspectives. Allowing our beliefs to be challenged is how we grow as a person. Once our beliefs are challenged we are able to reflect on our views and determine if maybe it is time to adjust them. This also gives us the opportunity to learn something new or to look at the issue from the other person's perspective. Being open to being wrong allows for greater understanding and growth. We can learn more about the subject or try to understand the other person's perspective. We then can make changes to our own beliefs to choose proper alternatives.

Those who have already reached higher levels of mindfulness appreciate their views being challenged. It forces them to reevaluate their viewpoints to ensure they align with reality. One of our favorite quotes from Winston Churchill is, "When the facts change, I change my mind, what do you do?" So ask yourself, what do you do when the facts change? Keeping an open mind and allowing ourselves to change our beliefs throughout our lives leads to greater opportunities.

Everything changes. What we understand, how we feel, even things we think of as facts. These all change over time, with new information and more experience. It is how each of us reacts to these changes that makes a huge difference in our lives. Are we able to flow with it or do we resist it? Those who are able to flow with, accept, learn, and adapt to changes are happier and more successful. This is because change is constant, and in this modern age, changes are happening faster than ever. If we do not allow ourselves to change, we will never grow.

Remember what Einstein said, "Insanity is doing the same thing over and over and expecting different results." By becoming aware of our beliefs and patterns of conflict, we have the opportunity to make beneficial changes. If the same conflicts or types of conflict keep happening, we need to to reflect on the belief that is causing the conflict, and more than likely, make some changes to our viewpoint. If we are always having the same problem, we might be the one creating the problem. It is worth it to consider changing if it can help to build healthy relationships.

We also need to embrace the idea that sometimes we are just wrong, and we need to learn and ask for forgiveness. Admitting that we are wrong is hard, especially after we make a big deal over it. Being able to admit you are wrong is a big part of becoming a better person and living your best life. In these moments when you determine you are wrong, it is okay to admit it, apologize, and if necessary, express how you will do better next time.

Not only is admitting you are wrong and apologizing a means to let go of unnecessary negative emotions, learning to forgive others and yourself, is another important life-hack. Forgiving yourself and others has been shown in multiple studies to increase health and well-being. Carrying around anger and guilt takes a lot of energy. Learn to forgive others and more importantly forgive yourself. Forgiving yourself and others is a great tool to add to the Let It Go Toolbox.

In the article, "Forgiveness: Who Does It and How Do They Do It?", the authors discovered that people who were actively more inclined to forgive, tended to be more agreeable, more emotionally stable, and more in-touch with themselves. The article discusses how the act of forgiving can be learned by anyone, especially those who are willing to be honest and introspective with themselves. This is why Step 4 and 5 are so important. We need to turn our eyes inward and, with our new-found awareness, reflect on our own beliefs. We can then learn, change, and move forward.

Pretty much every article you will read about forgiveness states, "it is not easy to forgive." However, those same articles also emphasizes that forgiving ourselves and others is absolutely necessary for our own mental health and inner peace. Start reflecting on some of the grudges that you have been carrying around. It may be time to forgive and let go. Please, if you are dealing with very difficult issues and trauma, reach out to a trusted adult for professional help.

The activity for Step 5 asks you to reflect even more deeply on yourself. Take some quiet time to complete the activity. Remember to be open and honest with yourself. These questions are meant to help you better understand yourself and raise your self-awareness. These questions can be reused over time to see how your viewpoint and perspectives change.

Looking back allows us to be better judges of the situation. We can use this hindsight to learn, especially if we are willing to be completely honest with ourselves. Each of us have had difficult times where we were right and when we were wrong. How we handle difficult situations impacts our well-being, for better or worse. It's important to learn from the past and our mistakes. Once we have learned all we can learn, we need to forgive and let it go.

Having the self-awareness to realize why a conflict exists will reveal a lot about you. It may give you a lot to think about and reflect on. Why do I react the way I do when I am challenged? When we start to understand the "why" behind our behaviors, this is when we can start changing them for the better.

Now that we are beginning to better understand ourselves and why we feel challenged, we can relax our mind, body, and spirit even more. When we are wrong, we can admit our mistakes and learn from them. We will move on with our best selves in the lead. When we are right, we can give the other person the grace to be wrong or just chalk it up to life no always being fair.

We are able to accept the next-best alternative, or maybe wait til something changes and we can get the resolution we want.

When you are in a relaxed state of mind, body, and spirit, you are ready to more effectively deal with the situation at hand. Ready to deal with it as your best self - cool mind, calm body, and collected spirit. You've got this.

We are almost there! Let's take a quick review of the Let It Go process.

In Step 1 we realize that we are being challenged or threatened and as a result our Defense Cascade is engaging.

In Step 2, we notice how our mind, body and spirit are reacting to the Defense Cascade engaging.

In Step 3 we take a deep breath to get in-between the Defense Cascade and our rational thinking mind.

In Step 4 we engage introspection to learn more about ourselves so we understand why we are triggered.

In Step 5 we raise our awareness and open ourselves to new perspectives.

Now let's move to Step 6 where we begin to move forward by learning what we can from the situation and letting go of the rest.

Self-awareness provides great potential for new opportunities.

END QUESTIONS FOR CHAPTER 7

1. Why is remembering that we are all human so important in the forgiveness process?

_____

_____

2. Do you think learning how to forgive in high school will help you in adulthood? Why or why not?

_____

_____

3. Why do you think it is sometimes so hard to forgive?

_____

_____

4. Can you describe a situation where it is important to forgive and to not forget?

_____

_____

5. Can you describe a situation where it would be better to forgive and forget?

_____

_____

CHAPTER 7 QUOTE QUESTIONS

The anonymous quote from this chapter is:

"The better awareness, the better your choices.
As you make better choices, you will see better results."
— Anonymous

1. Why does becoming more self-aware lead to making better choices?

_____

_____

2. Reflect on an excellent choice you made. What happened? What steps did you take to make that choice?

_____

_____

3. Think about a not so great choice you made. What happened? What steps did you take to make that choice?

_____

_____

4. How does making better choices lead to living your best life?

_____

_____

My Personality Type
from 16personalities.com

Visit the website 16personalities.com and take the free online personality test. This is a very popular test that has been used by millions of people to give them a basic overview of who they are. Be open and honest, and then reflect below!

LET IT GO
Activity #4

Personality: _____

Letter Identifier: _____

Roles: _____

Strategy: _____

Strengths Summary

Weaknesses Summary

My Personality Type
from 16personalities.com
LET IT GO: Activity #4

Romantic Relationships Summary

Friendships Summary

Parenthood Summary

Career Paths Summary

Workplace Habits Summary

Personality Test Conclusion Summary

What Did you Learn from 16Personalities?

My Personality Type
from 16personalities.com
LET IT GO: Activity #4

Do you agree or disagree with 16Personalities, why?

What surprised you most, why?

What changes can you make in your life to start living your best life right now?

1. _____

2. _____

3. _____

Raise Our Self-Awareness

Increase your self-awareness by answering the following questions. Be open and honest with yourself as you answer the questions. Answer the question as your overall self and then answer each with the perspective of Mind, Body and Spirit.

Who am I, really?
Overall:
Mind:
Body:
Spirit:

How do others perceive me?
Overall:
Mind:
Body:
Spirit:

What do I need to change about myself?
Overall:
Mind:
Body:
Spirit:

What do I want most in life?
Overall:
Mind:
Body:
Spirit:

What am I doing about the things that matter most in my life?
Overall:
Mind:
Body:
Spirit:

What is life asking of me? What am I asking of myself?
Overall:
Mind:
Body:
Spirit:

Raise Our Self-Awareness
LET IT GO: Activity #5 Continued

Am I holding on to something I need to let go of?
Overall:
Mind:
Body:
Spirit:

When did I last push the boundaries of my comfort zone?
Overall:
Mind:
Body:
Spirit:

What worries me most about the future?
Overall:
Mind:
Body:
Spirit:

Raise Our Self-Awareness
LET IT GO: Activity #5 Continued

How do I want others to see me? Who do I want to be?
Overall:
Mind:
Body:
Spirit:

Do I treat myself right? Is my internal dialogue with myself kind?
Overall:
Mind:
Body:
Spirit:

Do I have any bad habits that need to change?
Overall:
Mind:
Body:
Spirit:

LEARNING TO FORGIVE OURSELVES AND OTHERS ALLOWS YOU TO LIVE YOUR BEST LIFE

August 1, 2023 | 3andB.com Staff Blog Post
FOR IMMEDIATE RELEASE

You, I, and probably every person around us have at some point experienced disappointment. You might feel disappointed due to unmet expectations, painful experiences, and even betrayal from yourself and others. Although it is quite difficult to deal with the sensation of disappointment, learning how to let go and offer forgiveness is often the best thing you can do. It is possible to let go of negative feelings, and I'm here to tell you how doing that can bring you great relief.

Why is forgiveness so important?

Holding grudges and placing blame is exhausting and causes more pain for you than anybody else. Keeping negative emotions in your mind and heart can even impair your health. Believe it or not, studies have shown that there is a link between forgiveness and health. Feeling hurt for a long time can affect your physical well-being and put your body in a fight-or-flight mode. For example, it can negatively impact your immune system, your blood pressure, and even the rhythm of your heartbeat. This can have long term effects, like frequent illnesses and cardiovascular diseases! So, why put yourself at such risk when there is another solution?

Yes, I know that it's not always so simple to offer forgiveness to someone who hurt you, even if (and sometimes especially) that person is you. Everybody makes mistakes, big and small. *Finding the will and strength to get over them can be quite hard, and finding the will and strength to get over them is quite difficult.* At the end of the day, we are all human and we will hurt each other, even if we didn't mean to. Offering forgiveness, even if you didn't get an apology, is the best way to live a happier and healthier life.

No, I'm not saying that you need to pretend that nothing happened or continue a relationship with somebody who hurt you very badly. But it is important to realize that getting hurt is a part of the process of growing up. Once you grasp the idea, you will see that forgiving is the best way to move forward. Setting yourself free from the burden of feeling angry at yourself or someone else will bring you such great relief that you'll wonder why you haven't done this earlier.

How do we forgive ourselves and others?

Now comes the part when you actually have to do the work, and I can't say that this is a straightforward process. There will be times when finding the strength to get rid of all the negative emotions will be really challenging, but remember – the sooner you are able to do this, the sooner you will feel the positive changes in your life. So, what exactly can you do?

1. First things first, face the emotions you're currently feeling. Try to see the bad experience from another perspective without feeling the need to blame anyone. You can even write your thoughts down to make it easier to work on them.

2. Next, ask yourself what you can do to work through them. Will going on a walk help, or perhaps spending your time doing something creative? Once you find your outlet, you'll notice that making changes will come easier.

3. This is perhaps the most important part – remember that we're all human, that making mistakes is part of a person's growth, and that offering forgiveness is important for moving forward in life. Try to let go of what happened in the past, focus on the future, and how you can improve it.

4. Remember what you've learned and incorporate it into your life. Forgiveness doesn't come instantly; instead, it is through daily practice that you will learn how to overcome negative feelings and get the burden off your shoulders.

Living your best life starts now

Whether you're trying to forgive a family member, a friend, or yourself, finding a technique that works well for you is the first thing you should do. Learning how to forgive during your high school years will make it easier for you to use this technique into adulthood. In addition, it will help you enjoy the freedom that comes from clearing the emotional burden you've been carrying for so long. Keep your energy clear, and embrace the peace and happiness that comes from letting go of negative emotions. Regain the positive attitude that will make your life easier – and happier!

FORGIVENESS ARTICLE QUESTIONS

1. Why is remembering that we are all human so important in the forgiveness process?

_____

_____

2. Do you think learning how to forgive in high school will help you in adulthood? Why or why not?

_____

_____

3. Why do you think it is sometimes so hard to forgive?

_____

_____

4. Can you describe a situation where it is important to forgive and to not forget?

_____

_____

5. Can you describe a situation where it would be better to forgive and forget?

_____

_____

DEFINE AND DESCRIBE

Forgiveness: _____

_____

Patience: _____

_____

Next-Best Option: _____

_____

Reevaluate: _____

_____

20-20 hindsight: _____

_____

Personal Growth: _____

_____

ADDITIONAL ACTIVITIES

CHAPTER 7 ONLINE RESOURCES

SCAN & GO!

Check out the 3andB.com website for this chapter, just scan the QR code for instant access! Our website contains more information about everything we are discussing, including templates to complete all the work!

Chapter VIII: Step 6 - Move Forward

Objective: Students will learn three approaches to moving forward - expressing needs and emotions in a controlled, respectful manner, redirecting suppressed reactions into constructive behaviors, and remaining calm and letting go. They will also learn techniques for identifying root causes of long-term problems, considering multiple perspectives, setting aside time to work on them, and respecting themselves and others while dealing with conflict. Additionally, students will gain a deeper understanding of how challenging beliefs can lead to personal growth and greater understanding.

Chapter 8 Overview

• Our reactions to circumstances are one thing we can control, demonstrating personal growth.
• Approaching situations as our best selves is important for living our best life.
• Three approaches to moving forward include expressing, suppressing, and calming.
• Expressing needs and emotions in a controlled, respectful manner is effective and can lead to finding solutions.
• Suppressing reactions should be redirected into constructive behaviors.
• Remaining calm and letting go is the best option for moving forward in many situations and can prevent escalating anger and aggression.
• Dealing with long-term problems requires identifying root causes, considering other perspectives, and setting aside time to work on them
• Putting our best selves forward and respecting ourselves and others is key to dealing with conflict.

Video and Audio Resources

https://3andb.com/let-it-go-high-school-chapter-8-step-6-move-forward/

Chapter 8 Video Introduction
Chapter 8 Audio and Article Audio

Readings & Activities:
1. Starter Activity
2. Chapter 8 Text
3. Chapter 8 End Questions
4. Chapter 8 Quote Questions
5. Chapter 8 Article
6. Chapter 8 Article Questions & Vocabulary
7. More Resources

CHAPTER 8 ONLINE RESOURCES

SCAN & GO!

CHAPTER 8 STARTER ACTIVITY: STEP 6 - MOVE FORWARD

In Chapter 8, we discover three effective strategies for handling challenging situations. First, we can choose to express our emotions in the best possible way. Second, we have the option to momentarily suppress our emotions until we feel prepared to take action. Lastly, we can opt to maintain a calm demeanor. Every individual may approach the situation differently, but by expressing, suppressing, or remaining calm as our best selves, we can effectively navigate difficult circumstances.

Continuously develop your Mind, Body, & Spirit to live your best life!

How do you typically convey your emotions? Does it effectively address issues?

_____

_____

In tackling tough situations, how have you collaborated with others to find solutions?

_____

_____

How could you use breathing techniques to remain calm while working through a difficult problem or misunderstanding with a frtiend?

_____

_____

In our hectic lives, it's easy to overlook the small wonders that bring us joy and fulfillment. But by embracing gratitude, we open our eyes to the abundance of good in our daily lives. Before exploring Step 6, take a moment to recognize and appreciate the people, places, and things that inspire gratitude within you today.

I AM GRATEFUL FOR THIS PERSON:

_____

I AM GRATEFUL FOR THIS TEACHER:

_____

I AM GRATEFUL FOR THIS FRIEND:

_____

I AM GRATEFUL FOR THIS PLACE:

_____

I AM GRATEFUL FOR THIS OPPORTUNITY:

_____

I AM GRATEFUL FOR THIS THING:

_____

"I am larger, better than I thought;
I did not know I held so much goodness.
All seems beautiful to me.
Whoever denies me, it shall not trouble me;
Whoever accepts me, he or she shall be blessed,
and shall bless me."

— Walt Whitman

Chapter VIII

Step 6: Move Forward

One of the few things that we genuinely can control is our reactions to circumstances. You might remember from Chapter 1 that Viktor Frankl said, "Between stimulus and response there is a space. In that space is our power to choose our response. In our response lies our growth and our happiness." We demonstrate our growth as a person by our reactions to the world around us. Our reactions ultimately define our happiness.

Approaching every situation as your best self is what Viktor Frankl is writing about when he says our responses demonstrate our own personal growth and the personal contentment we have achieved in our lives. Use the Let It Go process to become the person in the face of adversity that is able to behave in a calm, cool and collected manner. This will demonstrate your own personal strength, integrity, and resilience. It also creates the conditions for happiness to flourish.

With our mind calm, body cool, and spirit collected we are ready to look at the situation from varied perspectives. We are ready to deal with it as our best self.

In general, there are three approaches to moving forward from a situation as outlined by the American Psychological Association:

> The first is expressing.
> The second is suppressing.
> The third is calming.

Each of these three approaches, when used appropriately, are good ways to move forward from a difficult situation.

Our first option is expressing. Expressing our emotions in a constructive and respectful manner that does not harm others is a good way to move forward. The article, "Control Anger Before It Controls You" by the American Psychological Association states that expressing anger in an assertive, non-aggressive manner is healthy. When in a difficult situation, after taking a deep breath and relaxing so our best self emerges, we can clearly state our needs and how we would like our needs met. It is most effective to do this non-aggressively while respecting ourselves and all others involved.

Expressing ourselves in a controlled manner is a good method to dealing with a difficult situation, especially a situation that needs to be resolved immediately. Perhaps a fellow classmate is being impolite and is insulting your opinions and eventually resorts to personally insulting you. You have a thousand reasons to be triggered, angry, upset. Instead, you collect yourself and remain calm. When you talk to them you put your best self forward. In these type of situations, expressing that you are upset, why you are upset and offering a potential solution that could work for everybody can be really helpful. This is an example of stating your needs and how you would like them met. If you can do this non-aggressively and respectfully, you are way more likely to get what you need out of the situation.

Sometimes in life, it is not about getting what we want when we are in a difficult situation. It is about getting what we need. A lot of the time, what we want is an ideal but what we need is much more achievable. For example, we might really want to go to the movies with our friends, but what we actually need is to spend time with people we like and care about. Or we want to make plans we can count on, but what we need is to feel respected and included in any changes in those plans. As the previously mentioned article states, "being assertive doesn't mean being pushy or demanding; it means being respectful of yourself and others." Always allow your best self to emerge first and let it guide you. Nobody likes being yelled at or pushed around. We are all more likely to listen to someone calm.

When we calmly and clearly state how we are feeling and how we think it could be resolved, we are respecting ourselves. When we give the other person a chance to do the same thing, we are respecting them. For example, imagine a teacher has given you a low score on a test you felt you had done really well on. Explaining to the teacher that you thought you had done well, is a good start. Asking if there is a way to take a re-test or get some extra credit gives the teacher a chance to offer a solution that might help. They want you to succeed, too! It does not guarantee that it will turn out the way you want right now, but it sets the groundwork to work together in the future to get better grades. If everyone does their best, that is all we can really expect from life.

We know what you are thinking. Some people are just rude, inconsiderate, jerks. You are not wrong, but you do not need to stoop to their level. If you maintain your best self, you will not give them power over your responses or the satisfaction of getting a rise out of you. Maintain your best self at all times. Your best self is always going to be your best option. If the issue does escalate and an authority figure is brought in, or the issue needs to be resolved at a later date, you will be in a stronger position by having maintained your composure. You do not need to become a jerk just because you are dealing with one. Work on being your best self at all times!

Our second option is to suppress the reaction. Suppressed reactions should be converted or redirected into something constructive, if possible. The aim here is to redirect your emotions into a more constructive behavior. If we do not redirect that suppressed reaction into something constructive, we just end up bottling up our feelings which can have negative consequences later. Either by exploding at another time or by harming our health, both mental and physical. That is why it is important to always convert suppressed reactions into positive constructive behaviors.

If you enjoy expressing yourself through your clothes, a big change in the dress code at school can really be upsetting. Maybe your school starts a uniform policy or you end up going to a new school that only allows uniforms. By suppressing your anger, you can redirect it somewhere else. You could decorate the inside of your locker to show your personality, for example, or maybe create art that illustrates the importance of freedom of expression. Maybe you could start running in the mornings to process the frustration. There are many ways to to channel feelings of anger, frustration and/or powerlessness into something constructive!

Pro-tip: journaling is a great way to redirect and express yourself in a way that will help you remain calm!

Lastly, our third and perhaps best option, we can take a deep breath, remain calm, and not get mad. Here, we could not agree more with the American Psychological Association when they state - "remain calm and let it go." Sure you are disappointed about a recent rule change from school administration. Yet, you choose to remain calm. You take a moment to think about why the change was made, recognize that while it might be negative for you it could be really positive for others. As much as we might wish it was, not everything is about us and that is okay. By choosing to accept the situation as it is, you are helping others as well as yourself. You have learned to accept life and the many things that are simply beyond our control.

The activity for Step 6 asks you to identify when it is best to express, suppress, or calm. Explore each of the scenarios and determine what works best for you. There is no right or wrong answer. We want you to reflect on using these tools so you are ready to utilize one of those options when you need it.

In case you were wondering, scientists also studied the consequences of "letting it rip" or freaking out. In almost all cases, freaking out actually escalates the anger and aggression, and does not assist you or the person you are confronting in resolving the situation. Are you more likely to give a person what they need if they ask for it respectfully or if they are freaking out?

Step 6 is about moving forward. So what about real problems in our lives that we cannot escape? How do we move forward? We need to face them, as our best self, in a calm, cool and collected manner so we can use all of our resources at our disposal to aim for the best outcome.

Problems at school, difficulties at home and health issues are very real and can go on for a long time. It is natural to become angry at these problems, especially when they are out of your control. Still, we have to deal with these things, even when we are not at fault. Taking time to apply these steps to the longer term problems we experience can help us be our best selves, especially when new short term challenges pop up. Dealing with longterm issues in any other way will do nothing but create more anxiety and stress in our lives, which will likely lead to even more problems.

Making time each day or each week to deal with longer term problems is the key to managing them with less stress. Worrying about a problem throughout your day does not make the problem any better. Dealing with the problem for a time period and then letting it go for the rest of the day is far more effective. By dealing with the problem head-on, we can let it go for the rest of our day.

When dealing with long-term problems it is important to deal with the real issue and not the drama surrounding it. This is where Steps 4, 5 and 6 can really help. Reflecting on what the root cause of the problem appears to be and why it bothers us is a good place to start. Think about other perspectives around the problem, which might help identify the root cause of somebody else's behavior and why they are doing that particular thing. Then figuring out whether expression, suppression or letting it go calmly will be the best tool. It is likely it will be a combination of those techniques. Make sure you set aside time daily or weekly to work on the longterm issues, so you can feel safe setting them aside the rest of the time. It will allow you to be more fully present and better able to deal with all the other stuff that comes up in your life.

If you feel overwhelmed or unsafe, seek out a trusted adult like a teacher, counselor or parent to help you. They may be able to offer you extra resources or professional assistance. Professionals are trained to come up with solutions, maybe some you had not thought of.

Moving forward with a calm mind, cool body and collected spirit makes all the difference in dealing with conflict. From a place of understanding and better perspective, we can learn from the moment and move forward with a new plan. We can choose to express, suppress, or calm when we find ourselves in a difficult situation, always putting our best self forward, respecting ourselves and others.

Let's review before moving on to the final step in the Let It Go process.

Step 1 asks us to realize we are entering the Defense Cascade after we have been challenged or threatened.

Step 2 asks us to notice how our mind, body, and spirit are reacting to the Defense Cascade engaging.

Step 3 asks us to take a deep breath so our thinking mind can take back control from our activated defense system.

Step 4 asks us to engage introspection to learn more about ourselves so we understand why we are triggered.

Step 5 asks us to raise our awareness and open ourselves to new perspectives.

Step 6 asks us to move forward by either expressing, suppressing, or calming.

And now, for the final step where we will Let It Go.

Whether you express, suppress, or calm - do it as your best self.

END QUESTIONS FOR CHAPTER 8

1. The American Psychological Association outlines three approaches to moving forward: expressing, suppressing, calming. Explain each.

Expressing: _____

_____

_____

Suppressing: _____

_____

_____

Calming: _____

_____

_____

2. Do you agree that remaining calm is the best option out of the three listed above? Why or why not?

_____

_____

_____

_____

3. Can you think of a time when something that used to make you really mad just did not bother you anymore? If so, why do you think your reaction changed? If not, how do you think you could accomplish that change, now that you have more tools for handling difficult situations?

_____

_____

_____

4. Can you think of a time when you were able to succeed in expressing your anger productively? If so, describe it. If not, explain how you think using the expression tool could help in the future.

_____

_____

_____

5. What activity do you think would help you the most when suppressing and redirecting your anger?

_____

_____

_____

CHAPTER 8 QUOTE QUESTIONS

Walt Whitman is considered to be one of the greatest American poets. His poetry is known for celebrating nature, love, friendship and freedom of human expression. His most notable work, Leaves of Grass, is a celebration of life. The following is a quote from the book:

"I am larger, better than I thought;
I did not know I held so much goodness.
All seems beautiful to me.
Whoever denies me, it shall not trouble me;
Whoever accepts me, he or she shall be blessed,
and shall bless me."

1. Using the internet, describe who you think Walk Whitman was. Why do you think he has become one of the most influential American poets?

_____

_____

2. What do you think Walt Whitman meant when he said, "I am larger and better than I thought, I hold so much goodness"?

_____

_____

3. How do you think Walt Whitman handled it when someone did not like him?

_____

_____

Moving Forward Using Express, Suppress, and Calm.

Read the scenario. After learning about the Let It Go process, write out how you would respond as your best self using express, suppress, and calm.

LET IT GO
Activity #6

Scenario 1: You did not understand the lesson very well. Now you are frustrated and can not complete the homework.

How do you handle the situation using?

Express:	Suppress:	Calm:

Scenario 2: Guests spent the night in your house. After they leave you discover your room is a wreck and some toiletries like your toothpaste have disappeared.

How do you handle the situation using?

Express:	Suppress:	Calm:

Scenario 3: You spent 10 minutes waiting for fast food at the drive-thru window. After pulling away you realize you have the wrong order. You go inside.

How do you handle the situation using?

Express:	Suppress:	Calm:

Scenario 4: You worked extremely hard for your employer this year and were told by your employer to expect a "good" holiday bonus. Instead, you receive a gift card to a coffee shop.

How do you handle the situation using?

Express:	Suppress:	Calm:

Scenario 5: Someone in the school is spreading lies about you online.

How do you handle the situation using?

Express:	Suppress:	Calm:

Scenario 6: The teacher calls you up to their desk. They have decided to give you a zero after someone stole your work from the basket to copy it.

How do you handle the situation using?

Express:	Suppress:	Calm:

HOW TO CHANNEL ANGER AND FRUSTRATION INTO POSITIVE ENERGY AND BEHAVIORS

August 1, 2023 | 3andB.com Staff Blog Post
FOR IMMEDIATE RELEASE

Have you ever felt so angry that all you want to do is scream and break things? This is what pure RAGE feels like. Chances are, you're familiar with this feeling.

While this is a pretty extreme example, everyone gets at least a little bit angry from time to time. Most people get angry somewhere between a few times a week to a few times a day. There's a big range of intensity from mildly annoyed to being ready to go on a full rampage, and it's perfectly normal to experience the whole spectrum.

Sometimes things just don't go your way, or someone does something horrible. Any number of things can cause anger and frustration. What's much more important than how you feel however is what you choose to do about it.

Anger Is Neutral. Only Your Response To It Can Be Positive Or Negative.

While anger is perfectly normal to experience, it can be a majorly destructive emotion if you don't learn how to mediate your reaction to it. Anger has led to some of the worst moments in human history! It clouds a person's judgment and allows us to make decisions we later regret. Would a calm and collected person be easily provoked into hurling insults and throwing things? Probably not! If they were, it would be embarrassing and hurtful. These extreme behaviors only tend to manifest when we've lost control of our regular decision-making processes in the midst of a wave of emotion. This is what we want to avoid.

Repressing Anger Is Bad For Your Health.

Another toxic effect of anger can actually come about when we hold it in instead of expressing it constructively. Repressing anger can be just as bad as letting it out in destructive ways. When you bottle it up, it not only feels terrible, but it can actually be harmful to your health as well. Repressed anger can lead to passive-aggressive behaviors, depression, anxiety, headaches, and sleep disorders.

136

So if you can't let your anger out by throwing a tantrum, and you shouldn't bottle it up, what exactly should you do?

Learn How To Channel It Into Something Positive.

Anger can actually be an incredibly useful emotion. When you feel it simmering, it's usually there for a reason. Some common triggers for anger are experiencing injustice, feeling powerless, frustrated, or maybe even being threatened. You're probably feeling it for a good reason, and it's likely something you need to address.

While some of the worst moments in history were shaped by anger, so were some of the best ones. Anger is the spark that started countless civil rights movements all over the world. It's a powerful emotion that gives ample amounts of energy to be harvested for either good or bad outcomes. It all comes down to learning how to control your anger and direct it into the right channels.

So how do we do this? How To Channel Your Anger Positively:

1) Recognize The Emotion

To start, you need to recognize your anger rising before it gets out of hand. Those first few moments when the feeling is just starting to bubble up is much easier to handle than after it becomes a volcano of rage.

If you feel your heart rate quickening and your breath becoming shallow, you may be going into fight-or-flight mode. This means your stress hormones are elevated and your body is preparing to deal with what it sees as a threat. You'll have trouble functioning well in this situation since your brain is stuck in survival mode and almost incapable of calm, thoughtful conversation at this point.

2) Create Space

After you recognize yourself losing control, you need to create some distance between yourself and whatever's triggering you. If it's something online, close your computer or turn off your phone. If it's someone you're having a conversation with, let them know you're done with the conversation for now and move into another room if possible.

It's helpful to create both physical space, and mental space between yourself and the stimulus that's upsetting you. Maybe try going for a walk, getting some fresh air, or distracting yourself by listening to music. Try your best not to overly focus your thoughts on what's bothering you, at least temporarily, since this will only add fuel to the flames of your anger.

3) Do Something Active

Doing something active can be a great way to both calm yourself down and channel your energy into something positive. Did you know your body actually becomes stronger when you're experiencing anger? Why not use that to your advantage and let out some steam by hitting the gym, going for a run, or even dancing your frustrations away!

4) Try To Relax

Trying to be calm in the middle of a heightened state is likely a lost cause, but after you've spent a few moments letting the anger move through you, you'll likely be able to start to relax. The nervous system is in a state of heightened activity when you're experiencing anger. You can use relaxation strategies like breathing exercises or meditation to calm your nervous system back down afterwards and you'll find that your anger naturally subsides along with it.

5) Reassess The Problem And Seek Help If You Need It

This step could be tricky, but once you're in a calmer state you'll be much more adept at figuring out why a trigger was making you angry, and what you can do about it. Great tactics for solving this problem can be journaling, talking to a friend, or even seeking out the help of a trusted adult like a teacher, parent or counselor. Even if you don't come to a solution right away, just expressing your frustrations and taking action may already help you feel a bit better about the situation.

Being angry is never pleasant, but you shouldn't ever feel bad about yourself when it comes up. Anger is just an emotion that comes and goes like any other feeling. It may be overwhelming at the moment, but if you incorporate the tactics we've discussed you'll be well on your way to channeling it wisely. Be patient with yourself. No one is perfect and we all say or do things we regret at some point or another when experiencing strong emotions. In time, you'll find yourself being less reactive, and quicker to calm down. Practice makes perfect might be a cliché saying. In truth, practice is how we get better at something, and that is worthwhile all on its own.

ANGER INTO POSITIVITY ARTICLE QUESTIONS

1. How often do you get angry? Do you feel like you are able to manage it well? Why or why not?

_____

_____

_____

2. Why is repressing your anger bad for your health?

_____

_____

_____

3. Why is it important to create a safe space for yourself when you are angry?

_____

_____

_____

4. How can doing something active help you deal with anger?

_____

_____

_____

5. How will you incorporate daily introspection into your life?

_____

_____

_____

ADDITIONAL ACTIVITIES

Check out the 3andB.com website for this chapter, just scan the QR code for instant access! Our website contains more information about everything we are discussing, including templates to complete all the work!

CHAPTER 8 ONLINE RESOURCES

SCAN & GO!

DEFINE AND DESCRIBE

Repressing Emotions: _____

_____

Confrontations: _____

_____

Relaxation: _____

_____

Expressing Emotions: _____

_____

Suppressing Emotions: _____

_____

Calming Emotions: _____

_____

Deep Breathing: _____

_____

Chapter IX: Step 7 - Let It Go

Objective: The objective of Step 7 is to learn how to let go of problems and emerge as our best selves. By understanding the Let It Go process and incorporating daily practices such as gratitude, smiling, and positive thinking, students can develop the skills needed to manage any situation. This will allow them to become more self-aware and confident individuals. This will also help them in dealing with difficult situations as their best self.

Chapter 9 Overview
• Step 7 of the Let It Go process involves making a conscious decision to let go of a problem and let the best self emerge.
• The greatest superpower is the ability to choose one thought over another, leading to positive outcomes.
• Letting go is a process of the mind, body, and spirit, involving self-awareness, reflecting on oneself, and using tools for dealing with emotions.
• Professional help may be necessary in dealing with trauma or difficult situations.
• Three daily practices that improve the ability to manage any situation and live one's best life are gratitude, smiling, and maintaining a positive mindset.
• Through the Let It Go process and daily practices, individuals become more self-aware and confident, able to face difficult situations calmly.

Video and Audio Resources

https://3andb.com/let-it-go-high-school-chapter-9-step-7-let-it-go/

Chapter 9 Video Introduction
Chapter 9 Audio and Article Audio

Readings & Activities:
1. Starter Activity
2. Chapter 9 Text
3. Chapter 9 End Questions
4. Chapter 9 Quote Questions
5. Chapter 9 Article
6. Chapter 9 Article Questions & Vocabulary
7. More Resources

CHAPTER 9 ONLINE
RESOURCES

SCAN & GO!

CHAPTER 9 STARTER ACTIVITY: STEP 7 - LET IT GO

In Chapter 9, we discover the importance of putting things into perspective and letting go. Whether it's a temporary issue or a long-term problem, we learn to forgive and release it. We understand that sometimes it's best to temporarily let go until we're ready to handle the problem as our best selves. As we develop our mind, body, and spirit, we realize that staying calm and being our best selves is the most effective approach to all situations, both positive and negative. By practicing the art of letting go in our daily lives, we gradually become the best versions of ourselves.

Continuously develop your Mind, Body, & Spirit to live your best life!

Why do you believe the authors think your ability to choose one thought over another is your most powerful superpower?

_____

_____

What are the mental and physical impacts of holding onto an old grudge?

_____

_____

How could you benefit from letting go of negative emotions?

_____

_____

In our hectic lives, it's easy to overlook the small wonders that bring us joy and fulfillment. But by embracing gratitude, we open our eyes to the abundance of good in our daily lives. Before exploring Step 6, take a moment to recognize and appreciate the people, places, and things that inspire gratitude within you today.

I AM GRATEFUL FOR THIS PERSON:	I AM GRATEFUL FOR THIS TEACHER:	I AM GRATEFUL FOR THIS FRIEND:
_____	_____	_____

I AM GRATEFUL FOR THIS PLACE:	I AM GRATEFUL FOR THIS OPPORTUNITY:	I AM GRATEFUL FOR THIS THING:
_____	_____	_____

"The more you talk about it, rehash it, rethink it, cross analyze it, debate it, respond to it, get paranoid about it, compete with it, complain about it, immortalize it, cry over it, kick it, defame it, stalk it, gossip about it, pray over it, put it down or dissect its motives it continues to rot in your brain. It is dead. It is over. It is gone. It is done. It is time to bury it because it is smelling up your life and no one wants to be near your rotted corpse of memories and decaying attitude. Be the funeral director of your life and bury that thing!"

— Shannon L. Alder

Chapter IX

Step 7: Let It Go

Welcome to Step 7, where we take matters back into our own hands. It is time to make a conscious decision to Let It Go and let our best self emerge. We embrace our best self by raising our awareness. We take the time to breathe, relax, put the problem into perspective, learn what there is to learn, then Let It Go. If it is something temporary, we Let It Go for all time. If it is an issue that will require more attention, we Let It Go for the time being until the right moment to deal with it arises.

Remember the phrase we love so much at 3andB:

**Your greatest superpower is your ability
to choose one thought over another.**

You too can become a hero! Use this superpower and select the thoughts that lead to your best self always emerging, regardless of the situation. Consistently selecting positive thoughts and remaining calm will lead to more positive outcomes.

As we have read, letting go is a process of the Mind, Body, and Spirit. We will become more self-aware as a person as we learn more about ourselves. As we practice the steps, and find what works best for us, we will be able to face all of life's moments. This includes the difficult moments that life throws our way.

The goal of the Let It Go process is to use these 7-steps to create a healthy, habitual type of response. With practice the 7-steps will become natural and automatic like your Defense Cascade. Let It Go will become a life-tool ready to be used in any situation that is good, bad, or ugly. Utilize the 7-steps and your best self will always emerge. You will always emerge with your mind calm, your body cool, and your spirit collected. Whether you decide to express, suppress, or calm, you can resolve difficult situations more easily and with less stress.

Letting go is not always easy. There are many ancient and modern pieces of wisdom to help with the process. Here we have brought together a selection of different tools that you can use as a base for adding more skills. We encourage you to keep learning and opening yourself up to different methods of dealing with emotions.

Modern psychologists will tell you that letting go is a necessary process of recovery. Letting go can be difficult especially if we have allowed ourselves to be defined by a particularly difficult situation, and it has become a part of our perceived identity. Letting go may also require us to change ourselves, the environment we live in, and those we choose to engage with. These types of changes are never quick or easy. Please, seek professional help if you need help dealing with trauma or other difficult situations. It can be overwhelming to handle it alone. This might include things like grief from the loss of a loved one, ongoing family conflict or health problems. Professionals are trained to help you. Reach out when you need them.

A large part of the Let It Go process, and for that matter growing as a person, is learning about ourselves. This is why Step 4 and Step 5 are so important. We need to make honest self-reflection a part of our daily lives. As we better understand our own beliefs, wants, needs, and motivations, we will gain more control over our lives. This will allow us to feel more confident about making changes that help us grow. Through daily self-reflection we become more self-aware. As we become more self-aware, we will be able to face difficult situations with confidence.

There is no need to keep holding onto many of life's trials once you have learned and grown from them. Appreciate the lesson for what it is and let it go. Free your headspace and energy to focus on your present. This will allow you to flourish in the future.

There are three other important daily practices that you can add to your life that will improve your ability to manage any situation and live your best life. These are so simple and yet so powerful.

The first is the power of gratitude. Each morning and before bed, take a few moments to be thankful for what you have and the people around you. Gratitude provides perspective because it makes you realize the good you already have in your life. Visit the 3andB website for an excellent gratitude journal that will help you keep track of all the things you are grateful for!

The second is easy. Just smile. Find moments throughout your day to smile. Wake up each morning and smile for a bit. During the day, take a moment to smile. Right before you get into bed for the night, leave the day with a smile. Give yourself moments to smile throughout your day, even if you do not necessarily feel like it. Smiling has been scientifically shown to release happiness chemicals in the body which greatly improve our mood, and increases positivity in our lives. Best of all, you can start this right now. (Did we just catch you smiling?)

Third, and the most important, is maintaining a positive mindset. This goes right back to our greatest super power, our ability to choose one thought over another. Begin by actively choosing positive thoughts over negative thoughts. You have the power. Time to own it!

Choosing positive thoughts, maintaining a positive mindset, being introspective, reflecting on ourselves, and letting go can be very powerful. These behaviors can create significant changes in our lives. Take it slow, open your mind to new ideas, and give yourself the time and space to digest them. Life and growth is a process. They both take time, patience, and effort.

As you begin to use the Let It Go process to reflect on your life each day, you will become increasingly aware of who you are and your beliefs. You will gain new levels of confidence. When you are challenged you will take it as an opportunity to question and strengthen or change your beliefs. As you begin to master these skills and yourself, you will become calmer in difficult moments. This will allow your best self to shine, rather than thoughtlessly reacting.

Ultimately, we may become humble enough to realize that our beliefs are not fixed and the human experience is just that, an experience. We can make the most of that experience by being grateful, positive, and reflective. Doing so will allow our lives to change and improve.

So here it is, the last step. Put the moment in proper perspective, learn what we can learn, forgive ourselves and others, and now… Let It Go.

Here are all seven steps, ready for you to utilize to deal with any situation. Congratulations for making it!

3andB
7-Step Process
to Let It Go

Step 1: Realize that you are challenged or threatened, a.k.a, mad, upset, angry, disappointed, jealous, or fill in whichever emotion or emotions that are causing you to feel mental anguish.

Step 2: Notice that your Defense Cascade response has been engaged and that your mind, body, and spirit are reacting.

Step 3: Breathe. Take a deep breath. Allow your breath to fill your body with energy and calm. This will disengage the Defense Cascade and allow your best self to reemerge.

Step 4: Engage introspection. As we learn more about ourselves, we understand why we are triggered.

Step 5: Awareness. Become fully aware of the trigger, as this provides perspective to learn from, change, or dismiss the threat.

Step 6: Move forward by expressing, suppressing, or calming your response to the threat, in a respectful, positive manner.

Step 7: Let It Go. Learn what there is to learn, place the entire moment in perspective, and Let It Go.

*Like learning an instrument, we must practice
self-awareness and letting go each day.*

END QUESTIONS FOR CHAPTER 9

1. What are the 7-steps to the Let It Go process:

STEP 1: _____

STEP 2: _____

STEP 3: _____

STEP 4: _____

STEP 5: _____

STEP 6: _____

STEP 7: _____

2. Why is it important to learn to Let It Go?

_____

_____

3. Do you feel like the entire Let It Go process will help you in your life? Why or why not?

_____

_____

4. Why is practicing gratitude important in order to live your best life?

_____

_____

5. Can you describe a situation where it would be better to forgive and forget?

_____

_____

6. What can smiling do for you?

_____

_____

7. Why is maintaining a positive mindset important to maintaining a healthy attitude?

_____

_____

8. According to Lee and John, the authors of this course, what is your greatest superpower and why?

_____

_____

8. What are some of the things you will do to live your best life?

_____

_____

_____

CHAPTER 9 QUOTE QUESTIONS

"The more you talk about it, rehash it, rethink it, cross analyze it, debate it, respond to it, get paranoid about it, compete with it, complain about it, immortalize it, cry over it, kick it, defame it, stalk it, gossip about it, pray over it, put it down or dissect its motives it continues to rot in your brain. It is dead. It is over. It is gone. It is done. It is time to bury it because it is smelling up your life and no one wants to be near your rotted corpse of memories and decaying attitude. Be the funeral director of your life and bury that thing!"

Shannon L. Alder is a life coach, therapist and author. She is focussed on helping her clients and readers live their best lives by helping them move on from difficult life situations. Now that you have learned the entire Let It Go process, why is Ms. Alder's quote so relevant? Write a short answer .

_____

_____

_____

_____

_____

_____

_____

_____

_____

What are you grateful for?
What makes you happy?
What are your life's dreams?

Fill each of the 33 boxes! Fill them in with things you are grateful for, that make you happy, and that you dream of achieving.

LET IT GO
Activity #7

Reflect on these and smile every day!

What are you Grateful for, why?

Grateful-1	Grateful-2	Grateful-3
Grateful-4	Grateful-5	Grateful-6
Grateful-7	Grateful-8	Grateful-9
Grateful-10	Grateful-11	Grateful-12
Grateful-13	Grateful-14	Grateful-15

What makes you happy?

Happy-1	Happy-2	Happy-3
Happy-4	Happy-5	Happy-6
Happy-7	Happy-8	Happy-9

What are your life's dreams or goals?

Dreams/goals-1	Dreams/goals-2	Dreams/goals-3
Dreams/goals-4	Dreams/goals-5	Dreams/goals-6
Dreams/goals-7	Dreams/goals-8	Dreams/goals-9

LEARNING TO LET IT GO LEADS TO YOUR BEST LIFE

August 1, 2023 | 3andB.com Staff Blog Post
FOR IMMEDIATE RELEASE

It is easy to feel overwhelmed by the pressures and stress of everyday life as a high school student. From assignments and relationships to extracurricular activities, there always seems to be something that demands your emotions, time, and energy. All these responsibilities can cause you to lose your cool and prevent you from living your best life.

However, there is a way to live a happier and more fulfilled life during high school and into adulthood. Learning to let go is an essential tool that will help you achieve your best life in adulthood. You can free yourself from unnecessary baggage by letting go of material possessions, old grudges, and bad habits.

Why It's Tempting To Carry Unnecessary Baggage And The Price You Pay For It

As a student, it is easy to imagine accumulating material possessions, engaging in bad habits, and holding onto grudges as not a big deal. You may think that you are young and that these behaviors will not significantly impact your life. However, carrying all that baggage can negatively impact your high school years and your future well-being.

Most high schoolers hold onto grudges to avoid uncomfortable communication, garner a sense of control or power, or provoke guilt in others. However, bitterness and anger are long-term consequences of holding onto grudges. Resentment can also lead to decreased motivation and focus, affecting academic performance and overall success. Engaging in bad habits such as substance abuse, procrastination, overeating and unhealthy relationships can also affect your life negatively.

- Procrastination, for instance, decreases your overall productivity, and limits your ability to reach your full potential.
- Unhealthy relationships can affect your mental and physical health.
- Unnecessary smoking, drinking, and binge eating can increase the risk of mental and physical health problems like obesity, depression, high blood pressure, and heart disease.

Lastly, accumulating excess material possessions can give you a false sense of security and lead to having feelings of superiority complex and entitlement. Remember, material possessions can bring you temporary happiness, but in the long run, these things can result in dissatisfaction and an endless cycle of wanting more. Being materialistic can distract you from having meaningful relationships, personal growth, and experiences, which may lead to an unfulfilled life.

How To Let It Go and Live Your Best Life as A High Schooler

Holding onto grudges, material things, and bad habits can have significant and lasting consequences. Letting these things run your life leads to stress, anxiety and unhappiness. They can also affect your relationships, academic performance and overall success. Releasing all of this unnecessary baggage can give you back control over your life and lead you toward achieving your best life.

If you are unsure how to untangle yourself from unnecessary baggage, here are some tips to help you let it go.

Identify Your Needs and What Is Holding You Back

The first step to "letting it go" is acknowledging that you are holding on to whatever "it" might be. The part of this step is to recognize what unmet needs are triggering you to engage with bad habits, hold on to a grudge or seek out lots of material possessions. What causes you to hold onto these habits? Are you bored, stressed, or chasing pleasurable feelings? Understanding your emotional and environmental triggers is the first step toward "letting it go."

Practice Self Awareness

Next, evaluate your emotions and reactions accurately. Determine if the behaviors or emotions are helping you or making the situation worse. Through self-awareness, you can learn important lessons and make better decisions in the future. For instance, if you want to relieve stress through substance abuse, ask yourself if there are alternative ways of reducing stress. Conversely, if you constantly have arguments with your friends, ask what the common denominator of those arguments is really about.

Release The Old Grudges

Notice how the grudges affect you. Are you constantly irritated by the person's presence? Do you sit and stew on what happened? Do you find yourself rehearsing what you would say to the individual if an opportunity presented itself? If so, this may indicate that you are still stuck in the past. Holding onto resentment and anger will harm you in the long run. Therefore, instead of disrupting the relationship or making it more awkward, you can practice forgiveness and choose to release the negative emotions.

Focus On the Present Moment

Living in the moment means that you do not worry about what happened in the past or what will happen in the future. By focusing on the present moment, you are able to appreciate and live in the present moment. You can practice living in the moment by:

- Mindfully listening to your lectures or friends without thinking of what you will say next.
- Being aware of your breath.
- Journaling things you are grateful for each day.
- Exercising mindfulness in everyday activities such as walking, eating, or reading.
- Creating a safe and healthy support system.

If you find it challenging to deal with a situation, remember that you can always contact family, friends, or counselors for assistance. Talking to someone you trust can help you process your emotions and guide you through decluttering or stopping bad habits. Remember that you don't have to face everything by yourself and that there are people who are happy to help.

Be Kind to Yourself

The last tip is to treat yourself with kindness and compassion. You are trying your best, and it is okay to make mistakes. Rather than focusing on your shortcomings, concentrate on your goals, strengths, and accomplishments.

Developing positive self-talk will help you build strength and confidence, making it easier to "let it go" when life becomes difficult.

LET IT GO ARTICLE QUESTIONS

1. How does focussing on the present allow you to let go of the past and stop worrying about the future?

_____

_____

_____

2. Why is it important to let go of old grudges in order to live your best life?

_____

_____

_____

3. How does being kind to yourself and others support your best life?

_____

_____

_____

4. Do you often procrastinate? Would a more structured form of time management be helpful for you to get things done on time? Why or why not?

_____

_____

_____

Chapter X: Conclusion

Objective: By practicing the Let It Go steps daily, high school students can develop emotional resilience and better cope with challenges, leading to improved overall well-being. Studies show that mindfulness practices, such as Let It Go, can reduce stress, anxiety, and depression, and enhance cognitive and emotional functioning.

Chapter 10 Overview
- Encourage students to practice the Let It Go steps daily.
- Short-term issues can be Let Go of quickly, but long-term issues need proper attention and a plan.
- If necessary, seek help from trusted family, friends, or professionals for long-term issues or if feeling overwhelmed.
- Learn to forgive others and oneself, practice gratitude, and choose positive thoughts over negative.
- Use Let It Go as a tool to become calm, cool, and collected during challenges and make better decisions.
- Believe in oneself and Let It Go.

Video and Audio Resources

https://3andb.com/let-it-go-high-school-chapter-10-conclusion/

Chapter 10 Video Introduction
Chapter 10 Audio and Article Audio

Readings & Activities:
1. Starter Activity
2. Chapter 10 Text
3. Chapter 10 End Questions
4. Final Reflection Activities
5. Final Presentation

CHAPTER 10 ONLINE RESOURCES

SCAN & GO!

CHAPTER 10 STARTER ACTIVITY: CONCLUSION

Chapter 10 concludes our exploration of self-discovery, equipping us to handle any challenge that comes our way. Whether it's a tough situation or just a regular day, we'll stay composed and tackle it with our best selves. By utilizing breathing techniques, we'll take a moment for self-care, releasing negative reactions and embracing positive behaviors that pave the way for improved solutions. Mastering the art of letting go in high school sets us up for navigating the inevitable difficulties of adulthood.

Continuously develop your Mind, Body, & Spirit to live your best life!

Do you think that learning to let go is a crucial skill for your success both now and in your future as an adult?

_____

_____

Why is it important to stay calm, cool, and collected at all times during high school and beyond?

_____

_____

Why is it important to seek professional help when overwhelmed by your emotions?

_____

_____

In our hectic lives, it's easy to overlook the small wonders that bring us joy and fulfillment. But by embracing gratitude, we open our eyes to the abundance of good in our daily lives. Before exploring Step 6, take a moment to recognize and appreciate the people, places, and things that inspire gratitude within you today.

I AM GRATEFUL FOR THIS PERSON:	I AM GRATEFUL FOR THIS TEACHER:	I AM GRATEFUL FOR THIS FRIEND:

I AM GRATEFUL FOR THIS PLACE:	I AM GRATEFUL FOR THIS OPPORTUNITY:	I AM GRATEFUL FOR THIS THING:

"One of the simplest ways to stay happy is letting go of the things that make you sad."

— Unknown

Chapter X

Conclusion

Thank you for reading Let It Go! Feel free to also thank your teacher if you learned something valuable. We hope you were able to take a couple of new skills with you on your journey.

Take time each day to practice the Let It Go steps. If you practice often and well, you will find yourself calmer in the face of confrontation. You will also feel more relaxed for having let go of a lot of stress and anger.

Remember, transitory or short-term issues can be Let Go of quickly. However, long-term issues will need proper attention and a plan. We must not dwell on long-term problems throughout our day as it will distract us from living in the present and moving forward. Each day or week, give long-term problems their assigned time. Ask for help from trusted family, friends, or professionals when you need it.

If you are holding on to a lot of anger, frustration or anxiety you can use Let It Go as a tool to start working through it. Some of us have a lot of experiences in our past that are very hard to let go of without help. If you have a difficult issue, you may need to seek professional help and counseling to work through it in order to let it go. This tool is meant to help you work through the everyday conflicts we encounter, use it as often as necessary and seek help from professionals, especially when feeling overwhelmed.

Learn to forgive others and most importantly, forgive yourself. Do not forget to practice gratitude each morning and evening, smile throughout your day and actively select positive thoughts over negative - calm mind, cool body, collected spirit - be that person!

Use Let It Go as a tool. Learn to become calm, cool and collected when challenged, and you will begin making better decisions that lead to a lot less anger, anxiety and drama in your life.

We believe in you! You got this. Now, Let It Go.

Join us at: 3andB.com

END QUESTIONS FOR CHAPTER 10

1. What is the most important thing you learned from this course?

_____

_____

_____

2. How do you plan to use Let It Go in your life?

_____

_____

_____

3. Of the 7 steps in the Let It Go process, which one is most important to you? Which one is most difficult for you?

_____

_____

_____

4. Are you ready to start Letting It Go?

_____

_____

_____

FINAL REFLECTION ACTIVITY

ESSAY TOPICS

Why is choosing one thought over another, choosing positive thoughts over negative, your greatest superpower?

How would you use Let It Go to improve your performance in-school, at-work, and while performing an after-school activity?

Why is forgiveness so important to maintaining a healthy life?

How do you plan to use breathing to maintain a positive attitude at all times?

How can smiling and practicing gratitude help you live your best life each day?

FINAL PRESENTATION

Create an 8 slide presentation. The presentation should focus on the 7 steps of the Let It Go program and what you have learned.

There is no possession more valuable
than a good and faithful friend.

— Socrates

Biographies

Lee Eyerman

Lee is passionate about helping others unlock their full potential by assisting them in discovering their life's passions and providing guidance to help them meet their goals. Lee believes each of us are beautiful and unique individuals with a grand personal purpose to be fulfilled. He is a lifelong proponent of career and technical education that includes life skills, soft skills, and most importantly, human behavior skills so people are prepared to thrive in adulthood. As an educator, Lee spent over 16 years teaching students career and life skills in order for them to find rewarding careers in the business and technology industries. Prior to teaching, Lee was a corporate attorney working in corporate mergers and acquisitions in NJ and NYC.

Lee holds a Bachelors of Science degree in Business Administration, a Masters of Education in Applied Behavior Analysis and a Juris Doctor degree in Law. He is retired in good standing from the State of NJ Bar, holds multiple teaching licenses and is currently preparing to sit for his Board Certified Behavior Analysis Certification.

Lee will use his education and experience to assist 3andB community members discover traditional and non-traditional educational opportunities in order for them to reach their goals as quickly as possible. Lee is excited about developing his mind, body and spirit further as part of the 3andB community.

John Hunt

John has been a science educator for six years, his Bachelor's is in secondary education. He has really enjoyed his time as a teacher and getting to know his students but now wants to go beyond the scope of the science curriculum. He wants to provide students with the tools to be successful and make the best of many situations, which involves controlling emotions and harnessing them for something greater.

He is also a human resource manager and nerdy-bodybuilder. He is now adding video editor, digital designer, and co-founder/CEO titles to his list of skills to help make this 3andBoat float. He also makes time for fun as a musician and guitar player. He plays in several bands in his local music scene.

He believes that we are all capable of many great feats. This requires desire, the will to act, and discipline to sustain and maintain progress. He hopes to get others passionate about improving themselves and the world around them. John is excited to learn and grow more through his 3andB journey and help others along the way. He is a firm believer in the GOYB (Get-Off-Your-Butt) Principle and the power of small and consistent habits building towards a better life.

For more information or to join our community:

3andB.com

THE END!

(YOU DID IT, NOW LET IT GO!)

Made in the USA
Las Vegas, NV
14 September 2023

77561154R00096